T0294707

THE
LITTLE
HISTORY
OF
BRISTOL

THE
LITTLE
HISTORY
OF
BRISTOL

MAURICE FELLS

First published 2021

The History Press
97 St George's Place, Cheltenham,
Gloucestershire, GL50 3QB
www.thehistorypress.co.uk

British Library Cataloguing in Publication Data.
A catalogue record for this book is available from the British Library.

ISBN 978 0 7509 9335 7

Typesetting and origination by Typo•glyphix
Printed in Turkey by Imak

CONTENTS

ABOUT THE AUTHOR

Maurice Fells is a born and bred Bristolian who has long been passionate about his native city's colourful and rich history. He loves delving into archives relating to Bristol's heritage and collecting brochures, magazines and other paraphernalia about the city's past.

He has held key editorial posts in regional newspapers, radio and television and is now a freelance journalist, author and broadcaster. Maurice can frequently be heard on West Country radio stations talking about local history.

Maurice now has thirteen books to his name. They include *Bristol Plaques, Clifton: History You Can See, The A-Z of Curious Bristol, The Little Book of Bristol* and *The Little Book of Somerset*, all published by The History Press.

INTRODUCTION

History lessons at school were far from riveting. To say they were dull is an understatement. Lessons seemed to revolve around the class repeatedly reciting from memory long lists of names of kings and queens, the order in which monarchs ascended to the throne and the dates of battles galore. If you made a mistake the history teacher would pinch one of your ears. Ouch!

The very mention of civic history evoked a mass groan from my school class, which provided 'Sir' with another opportunity to pinch our ears.

So I was delighted to be asked to write *The Little History of Bristol* because it meant that I could write a history book that would be compact but also packed with fascinating facts, colour, incidents and human interest stories from the Iron Age to the present day. In this book I have refrained from including what in my view are boring long lists, or even short ones for that matter, which are simply catalogues of names and dates. Neither does my book set out to be a definitive history of Bristol filled with dry and stuffy details about minor incidents. There are accounts though of local events, many of which had national and even international importance. This book is intended to be more of a 'gateway' to the story of Bristol over the last one thousand years or so. It is written complete with 'warts and all' in an informal way.

The story of Bristol is synonymous with that of the sea. It has long looked overseas for its prosperity. Bristol's close association with wine can be traced back to when Norman barons with their taste for French wines settled here after the Norman Conquest. They imported substantial quantities of wine through the port. In medieval times explorers set out from Bristol in search of new lands. Today the Port of Bristol is a major centre for the importation of cars.

This book is not only a history but also a celebration of Bristol, which was the first borough outside of London to be made a county in its own right, sandwiched between Gloucestershire to the north and Somerset to the south. Later it became a city as well, making it the City and County of Bristol. It is a world apart with its own history, traditions and dialect. The most unusual feature of its dialect, unique to Bristol, is what is known as the 'Bristol L'. This is where the sound of the letter L is appended to words that end with the letter 'A'. America, for example, becomes Americal.

Civic history, by the way, doesn't need to be presented in a dull fashion. Hopefully a few unusual facts in this introduction will whet your appetite to turn the following pages. Let's begin with one from the 'Maire's Kalendar' that was compiled by Robert Ricart, a fifteenth-century town clerk. He recorded that one of his duties was to provide dice for the Mayor and councillors when they were killing time waiting for people to arrive.

The duties of the Mayor and councillors didn't just include attendance at meetings. Once a year they went duck hunting at Trin Mills, now Bathurst Basin. This was part of a ceremony known as Beating the Bounds – an ancient custom of inspecting the boundaries of a village, town or city. In Bristol's case this was a five-day perambulation on land and sea. On the first four days the city's dignitaries walked part of the boundary on foot, while on the fifth they boarded a vessel to take them to the islands of Steep Holm and Flat Holm in the Bristol Channel, 25 miles from the centre of Bristol. First-timers on the walk were bumped on marker stones along the route. Beating the Bounds had become such a popular ceremony that by 1900 a group of young women formed a volunteer bumping corps and were said to have dealt vigorously with many of the civic dignitaries. The last recorded duck hunt was in 1742, probably much to the relief of the birds.

From the natural history records we know that Bristol even had its own dinosaur known as thecodontosaurus. It lived on tropical islands in the Bristol area during the Triassic period around 210 million years ago. Fossilised bones of a thecodontosaurus were found in a quarry on Clifton and Durdham Downs in 1834. It was the fourth species of dinosaur to be identified anywhere in the world.

Through the centuries Bristol has witnessed wars, plagues and riots, and has been at the forefront of the discovery of new lands. Bristolians have also had a ringside seat at many events of national importance including the launch of the world's first iron-hulled propeller-driven ship, the building of the world's first Methodist Church and, more recently, the maiden flight of the world's first supersonic airliner.

Fascinating nuggets of information about Bristol's long and diverse history from the Iron Age to the present day can be found on every page of *The Little History of Bristol.*

Maurice Fells, 2021

ACKNOWLEDGEMENTS

Writing books about Bristol is for me a labour of love but they only get published with the help of many other people. Firstly, I must thank Nicola Guy, Local History Commissioning Editor at The History Press, for asking me to write *The Little History of Bristol*. Then I need to thank the team of editors and designers who turn the grey mass of my typed manuscript into a truly presentable book.

I started researching *The Little History of Bristol* by delving into my own archives of old newspapers, press releases and other publicity material that I have accumulated while working as a journalist on newspapers, radio and television. Local knowledge and my curiosity about anything connected with Bristol have also played a big part in the research process.

I have made many visits to the Reference Section of Bristol Central Library, where the staff have not only dealt patiently with my many enquiries, some of them most obscure, but have also shown an interest in the book I was writing. In particular, I mention Dawn Dyer, whose knowledge of historic Bristol seems unrivalled.

The illustrations in this book are the work of two Bristol artists: Samuel Loxton (1857–1922) and Frederick George Lewin (1861–1933). Loxton was born in Clifton and became an architectural draughtsman and surveyor. He became known for about 2,500 drawings of buildings in Bristol. Much of his work appeared in the *Bristol Observer*. Lewin, who lived in Redland, was originally a journalist but later decided to become an artist. The drawings of both these artists are reproduced here by kind permission of the reference section of Bristol Central Library.

A special thank you goes to two extremely good friends, Janet and Trevor Naylor, who have given me so much help in many different ways, including carefully reading my typed manuscript and pointing out glaring errors and coming up with good ideas.

1

A ROYAL CITY
AND COUNTY

The growth in Bristol's wealth and its significance as a thriving trading centre has long been underlined by the number of royal visits the city has hosted over the centuries. In the early days one of the principal royal visitors was King John, who was recorded as having made nineteen visits. Most of them would have been to carry out business at the castle. Henry II spent four years here as a boy, under the care of his uncle, Earl Robert of Gloucester, who provided him with a tutor. Later he held a council in Bristol and granted a charter to the burgesses, allowing them to choose a Mayor from among themselves.

Henry III held his first council at Bristol Castle, while Edward I twice spent Christmas here. Records show that there were more than fifty visits made by members of the royal family between 1200 and 1900.

When King Henry VII was in Bristol he imposed a most unusual levy on the city's menfolk. He ordered everyone who was worth £20 to pay him 20*s* because 'their wives were sumptuously apparelled'. The King obtained a total of £500 in levies.

PUTTING OUT THE RED CARPET

No expense seems to have been spared when Queen Elizabeth I spent a week in Bristol in 1574 on one of her royal progresses around her realm. She was most lavishly and loyally entertained by the city dignitaries. The Queen entered Bristol riding side saddle on a white horse through one of the gateways in the medieval boundary wall. To ensure that she had a smooth ride, the rough roads had been specially covered in sand to provide a level surface. The blue velvet saddle cloth that the Queen used is now in the care of the Society of Merchant Venturers at the Merchants' Hall in Clifton, where it is kept in a glass case.

Her Majesty was greeted by the Mayor and other civic leaders as well as 400 infantrymen, including 100 pike men in white armour, all wearing new uniforms. A tour of the city started with a visit to the High Cross, where boys from the grammar school recited verses to Her Majesty. The highlight of the week was a mock sea battle between an English ship and a Turkish vessel staged at Trin Mills, now Bathurst Basin. Records describe it as being 'verie costlie and chargeable, especially in 'gonne-poudre'. Indeed, some £200 was spent on gunpowder alone for the guns that provided the royal salute. Unfortunately, shortly before Her Majesty arrived a store of gunpowder kept at the Pelican Inn on Victoria Street exploded. Ten men were killed and five others injured, with the pub being destroyed in the explosion.

During her stay, Elizabeth is reputed to have described St Mary Redcliffe church as 'the fairest, goodliest and most famous parish church in England'. But strangely no documentary evidence has ever been found – not even a single line in the church records – to support this remark. It seems curious that if the Queen had visited the church no one saw fit to make a note of it for posterity. Arguably, St Mary Redcliffe would not have been looking its architectural best as at the time about a third of its cloud-piercing spire was missing. It had been struck down in a storm in 1446 and was not replaced for another 426 years. When the spire was restored the Mayor, Councillor William Proctor Baker, laid its capstone, which was nearly 300ft above street level. He certainly had a head for heights, being hoisted part of the way up the spire in a makeshift lift consisting of boards, rope and cloth, and then climbing the rest of the way.

Queen Elizabeth and her large entourage of courtiers and maids were hosted by John Young at his Great House, which stood on what is now the site of the city's largest concert venue, the Colston Hall. John Young, who had laid on a banquet for the Queen, was later 'thanked' for his hospitality with a knighthood. But the royal visit still cost Bristol Corporation £1,053 14*s* 11*d*. Apart from paying for sand to cover the streets, there was a bill to pay for painting and gilding the High Cross that amounted to £66 13*s*.

As a souvenir of her visit, the Recorder of Bristol gave the Queen a purse containing £100 in gold.

It seems that mock sea battles were something of a set piece in Bristol's programme for entertaining royalty. When Anne of Denmark, the Queen of James I, visited Bristol in 1613 she too was entertained with such a spectacle. Afterwards she told the Mayor that she never knew she was Queen until her visit to Bristol.

In more modern times royal visitors carried out public duties. For example, the Prince of Wales opened Knowle Racecourse in 1873. The Prince, who was staying at Berkeley Castle, Gloucestershire, visited the course on each of the three days of the opening meeting. The race card included steeple chasing and flat racing over a course of a mile and three-quarters. It was estimated that there were more than 200,000 spectators over the three days. No doubt the attendance figures were boosted by the presence of the Prince. In 1891 the Duke of Edinburgh was in Bristol to be granted the Freedom of the City. After receiving the honour, the Duke officially opened a newly completed wing of Bristol General Hospital.

Nearly 400 years after Elizabeth I visited St Mary Redcliffe, Queen Elizabeth II followed in her footsteps in April 1956. The police estimated that 20,000 people had flocked to the church grounds and surrounding streets waiting to see the Queen, accompanied by the Duke of Edinburgh, enter and leave the church. The royal couple had been given a private tour of the parish church, which with all its grace and spaciousness is often mistaken by visitors for a cathedral. The church visit was the first of several engagements the Queen had in Bristol that day. It was her first official visit to the city since being crowned three years earlier.

After leaving the church, the Queen officially opened the city council's new administrative headquarters on College Green. It replaced a Georgian building on Corn Street, which for 125 years had served the needs of the council staff.

In her speech to civic dignitaries, council members and staff at the opening ceremony, the Queen acknowledged Bristol's long history, which she said was linked with the River Avon. 'For centuries men of Bristol have sailed down the river to voyages of discovery and in the pursuit of trade upon which your fortunes have been founded. Bristol has flourished by the enterprise of merchants and the skill and craftsmanship displayed through the materials they had brought back.'

In 1995, Elizabeth II returned to St Mary Redcliffe church, this time to attend a service for charity workers. As she signed the visitors' book, Her Majesty was asked by the Rev. Tony Whatmough if she remembered her first visit. The

Queen replied that St Mary Redcliffe was not the kind of church that you forgot once you had visited it.

A ROYAL ROUND-UP

Royal Charters are generally granted by the monarch on advice from the Privy Council to establish significant organisations such as municipal boroughs, universities and schools. Over the years the monarchy has granted more than a thousand charters. Bristol has probably had more than its fair share of these.

One of the earliest charters granted to Bristol was given by Henry II in 1171. The charter granted the men of Bristol the right to live in the city of Dublin 'ad inhabitanda'. It was a reward for the part the wealthy merchants had played in the invasion of Ireland.

In the charter the King stipulates that Bristolians can live in Dublin 'with all the liberties and free customs which the men of Bristol have at Bristol and throughout all my land'.

The charter, which measures 5in by 6½in, is on parchment with a fragment of the seal remaining in green wax. It is written right through, leaving no room for additions: a measure taken in those days to prevent fraud. This charter is the oldest document in the Dublin City Library and Archives and is kept in a purpose-made case in the strongroom.

It is also thought to be the earliest law to confer the rights of people in either Britain or Ireland to live in each other's countries. It is a law that has never been repealed.

One of the earliest-known church schools was attached to St Mary Redcliffe church. In 1571 church officials paid £65 7s 9d for Letters Patent from Queen Elizabeth I to set up a free Grammar and Literature School in the parish. It began teaching children in the Chantry Chapel then standing in the south churchyard. The school moved in 1762 into the church's Lady Chapel. From these humble beginnings the school has evolved through various incarnations into the present St Mary Redcliffe and Temple Church of England School, built in Somerset Square behind the church in 1967.

A charter granted to Queen Elizabeth's Hospital (QEH) by Elizabeth I in 1590 comes out of the safe each March to go on show as part of the school's Charter Day celebrations. Written in Latin, the charter states that the school 'shall be everlasting' and always be named after the Queen. One of the school's benefactors was John Carr, who became a wealthy man by making soap at his factories in Bristol and London. He left instructions that the school should be modelled on Christ's Hospital, London, which was set up for fatherless children and for those from poor homes.

Queen Elizabeth's Hospital opened with just twelve boys but as the number of pupils grew it eventually moved from the centre of the city to its present site on Brandon Hill Park. For many years the boarders wore traditional dress of long gown, yellow stockings and buckle shoes.

Peaches Golding belongs to one of the most exclusive clubs in the land. There are only ninety-eight members and all have the title of Her Majesty's Lord Lieutenant. It is an office steeped in history and tradition, having been created in 1546 by King Henry VIII to take over the military duties of the sheriff.

As the present Lord Lieutenant for Bristol, Peaches Golding is no longer tasked with the training of local men to lead against domestic insurrection and foreign invaders. But as the Queen's representative for the County of Bristol she carries out a range of civic duties on behalf of the Queen.

Peaches Golding is a native of South Carolina, but has lived in Bristol for thirty-five years. She is believed to be the first black woman to have been appointed a Lord Lieutenant in England and was appointed by the Queen in 2017.

2

EARLIER TIMES

Most historians agree that Bristol's history goes back a thousand years or so. Beyond that little seems to have been recorded in any kind of documentary form. However, we do know that the Saxons, Romans and Iron Age man trod the soil that is now part of the area often referred to as Greater Bristol. Most of the knowledge that we do have of those people comes mainly from archaeological excavations. There is evidence, for example, of settlements going back to the Palaeolithic era with 60,000-year-old archaeological finds at what are now the suburbs of Shirehampton and St Anne's. Stone tools made from flint, stone and quartzite have been found in terraces of the River Avon especially around Shirehampton.

MYTHS AND LEGENDS OF OLD BRISTOL

The vacuum of documentary information from times past has probably led to the creation of the many myths and legends about the foundation of Bristol. One legend credits two mythical Roman soldiers, Brennus and Belinus, with being its founders. They are said to have led an army to sack Rome in 391 BC before founding Bristol.

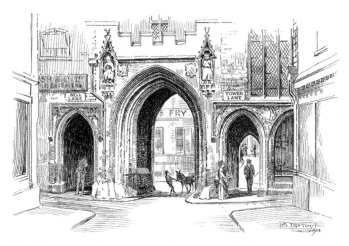

St John's Arch with the statues of Brennus and Belinus

Indeed, such was the belief in this story that in the fourteenth century stone statues of the couple were installed on either side of St John's Gateway in Broad Street, one of the portcullised archways that led through the city wall in the Middle Ages. Astride the arch sits the church of St John the Baptist, which once stood on the quayside of the River Frome, now culverted underneath the roads of the city centre.

The weather-beaten statues which are tucked into niches of the gateway still look down on passing pedestrians and traffic as they have done for more than 700 years. No one knows who carved the statues or who placed them there or when. Brennus is supposed to have brought wealth to the city and helped it grow. He and Belinus were said to have reigned as Kings of Britain. However, there is no evidence to suggest that either of these people existed. Sceptics of this tale point out that the seated statues of Brennus and Belinus depict them carrying crucifixes, though the brothers are supposed to have lived long before Christ.

A rather romantic tale about the creation of the Avon Gorge, one of Bristol's most spectacular tourist attractions, has been handed down from generation to generation. It features another pair of supposed brothers, Goram and Vincent, who were giants living on Clifton Down. They are both said to have fallen in love with Avona, a girl from Wiltshire. She is supposed to have instructed them to drain a lake that stretched from Bradford-on-Avon in Wiltshire to Bristol.

Goram is said to have started work on this mammoth task by digging a brook on the nearby Blaise Castle estate. Legend has it that he consumed too much beer and fell asleep. Meanwhile, Vincent dug the Avon Gorge and drained the lake, thereby winning the affection of Avona. Upon waking, Goram is said to have stamped his foot and thrown himself into the Bristol Channel. It is said that he turned into stone and left his head and shoulders above water as the islands of Flat Holm and Steep Holm, which lie between Weston-super-Mare and Cardiff. His body is now Brean Down, a promontory of the coast of Somerset.

One of many versions of this myth has it that the brothers were working together cutting through the carboniferous limestone of the Avon Gorge sharing just one pick and shovel, when Goram fell asleep. On waking he was accidentally killed by his brother's pickaxe. Apparently, Vincent did his share of the work in the morning and, when he finished his stint, threw the tools to his brother when the accident happened. Vincent is commemorated by St Vincent's Rocks in the Avon Gorge. The story goes that the Avon Gorge was named after Avona.

The reality of the creation of the Avon Gorge is less fanciful than any legend. It was probably formed during the last Ice Age, which ended 10,000 years ago, by the River Avon carving its way through the limestone. The river flows from

Bristol to the Severn Estuary through the Avon Gorge, a distance of about 7 miles. The gorge itself though is only 1½ miles long. Today it forms the boundaries of the unitary authorities of North Somerset and Bristol, with the boundary line running along the south bank.

Legend has it that the garden of an early Georgian Manor House was the setting for a deadly duel involving two men competing for the hand in marriage of a beautiful young woman.

The woman, who lived at Bishopsworth Manor House, was courted on a daily basis by her two suitors. However, she rejected the offer of both men and never left her home. However, the men could see her through the wrought iron garden gates as she strolled amongst the rose bushes.

Eventually she succumbed to the advances of one of her admirers and welcomed him into her home. He is said to have left his horse and spurs at the garden gate where they were seen by his rival, who then challenged him to a duel. This was a fight with swords that resulted in one of the men

Bishopsworth Manor

dying from a neck wound and the other being found lying on the terrace bleeding to death. It is said that the lady in question never married.

Bishopsworth Manor House, sitting on the southern fringe of Bristol, was once in the County of Somerset until boundary changes in 1930 took it into Bristol. The Manor House is a Grade II* building of around 1820 and is a two-storey private residence. It is crowned by a four-sided chimney arcade with the stacks linked to form a square in the style of Kings Weston House in north Bristol, which was designed by the celebrated eighteenth-century architect Sir John Vanbrugh. He is also well known for designing Blenheim Palace in Oxfordshire, the main residence of the Dukes of Marlborough, and Castle Howard, a stately home in Yorkshire.

THE 'TIME TRAVELLERS'

The dearth of knowledge about our Iron Age predecessors in Bristol did not deter BBC producer John Percival from launching a new television series in the 1970s seeking people willing to wear sheepskins for a year. Mr Percival and assistant producer Linda Cleave were most surprised when nearly 1,000 responses to their newspaper advert seeking people to take part in a series of programmes called *Living in the Past* arrived at the BBC studios in Bristol. Eventually twelve men and women along with three children, who were from the same family, were selected to take part in what the BBC described as a 'ground-breaking series'. In effect it was the first reality television programme.

The volunteers included teachers, a smallholder, a doctor, a nurse and a jobbing builder. They spent a year in a 'time-machine' that took them back twenty-three centuries in a bid to recapture how our ancestors lived in 300 BC. They moved onto a recreated settlement that the BBC built at a secret 5-acre site on the Somerset–Wiltshire border, well away from prying eyes. The 'settlers', wearing sheepskins and rough woollen clothes, ate, worked and slept just like Iron Age man. Their living accommodation was round wooden houses, the design of which carefully matched archaeological evidence. They looked after animals that lived in Iron Age times like small black cattle, pigs, goats, chickens and sheep from Soay, an islet in the Scottish archipelago of St Kilda. The 'settlers' grew primitive types of wheats, barley and beans. All their tools, clothes and equipment, from ploughs to the small bronze safety pins used to fasten the Celtic shawls, were meticulously copied from museum examples.

The volunteers had no television sets, radios, newspapers or books for the year. During this time they had no contact with the outside world. The only visitors allowed into the camp were the producer and his film crew recording how the families coped.

When the filming was completed the families simply resumed their normal daily lives, unlike those who take part in today's reality television programmes and seem to acquire instant celebrity status. The volunteers found that their bank accounts had been boosted by £1,000. They had each been paid £20 a week by the BBC. In 1978 *Living in the Past*, a twelve-part series, was broadcast on BBC 2 and attracted around 18 million viewers a week.

UPON OBSERVATORY HILL

During the Iron Age, people began to settle on higher ground and formed themselves into tribes. What better place for height than Observatory Hill, just above the Clifton Suspension Bridge, the highest plot of land in Bristol above sea level. The Dubonni Tribe settled on this strategic site 338ft above the high-water mark of the River Avon below. It gave them panoramic views of the surrounding area and looked across the Avon Gorge at two other hill-forts known today as Stokeleigh Camp and Burwalls, both on the Somerset side. The Observatory Hill camp, a sched-uled ancient monument, was surrounded on three sides by a wooden stockade on earth ramparts protecting the Dubonni from other groups. William Worcester, Bristol's very own topographer of the fifteenth century, described the ramparts as 'a large collection of great stones piled up and small ones scattered around'.

Worcester spent his life measuring buildings and streets all over the country simply by pacing them. His measure-ments, particularly those of churches, were said to be so accurate that restorers were able to make a ruined building look like the original.

The site of the Observatory Hill Iron Age camp has been much defaced by quarrying and the construction of foot-paths. The roots of veteran trees are damaging the hillfort but portions of its ramparts can still be traced.

Observatory Hill's main feature today is the privately owned observatory, one of only three working camera obscuras in the United Kingdom. The building was origi-nally a windmill that was damaged by fire in 1777 when the sails were left turning during a gale and caused the equipment to catch alight. The building was left derelict until 1828 when William West, an artist and amateur astro-nomer, rented the old mill for 5s (25p) a year as a studio. Next to the tower he built an astronomical observatory with a revolving dome and telescope to allow what he called 'unrestricted observation of the heaven'. Next to this was a room he equipped with various astronomical maps, globes and instruments.

Beneath the camera obscura is a 250ft-long passage, excavated by William West. It took him two years to cut his way through the carboniferous limestone rock to a natural cave on the cliff edge of the Avon Gorge. This was said to have been the home of the giant Vincent. Originally the cave could only be accessed via a steep and perilous path down the cliff face. William Worcester wrote that it took him '124 paces to reach the cave'.

They Came, They Saw, They Conquered

The Romans began their invasion of Britain in AD 43 and within about five years had reached much of the West Country including the Bristol area. Led by Vespasian, Commander of the Second Legion, the Romans set up a camp on Clifton Down near Clifton Suspension Bridge – much earlier this was the site of an Iron Age camp – although they had a bigger base at Gloucester. However, there is no evidence that Bristol was a Roman town like nearby Bath (Aqua Sulis) or Cirencester (Corinium Dobunnorum), although the remains of isolated Roman villas and numerous artefacts including human bones have been unearthed in various parts of the city. Coins of the later Roman emperors have occasionally been discovered near Clifton Observatory.

Archaeological excavations in the present suburb of Sea Mills in north-west Bristol revealed a pattern of streets, cemeteries and wharves. Fragments of coins, tiles and pottery have been found and in 1873 the tombstone of a Roman female was discovered. Sea Mills was the site of a port the Romans called Portus Abonae. It was built at the point where the River Trym, which rises in South Gloucestershire, flows into the River Avon. The Romans needed to be near a river crossing from England to the fortress they had built at Caerleon (Isca Silurum) in South Wales so they could transport soldiers, equipment and provisions.

Traces of the Roman road known as the Via Julia, which ran from Bath to Portus Abonae, can be seen on Clifton and Durdham Downs. A short length of the road is visible as a slightly raised grassy bank near Downleaze. The Roman Army built roads, which were usually straight, to help them continue with their conquest of Britain.

Tramp the streets of Sea Mills today and you'll find the only indication of the Romans' settlement here is in the names of some of the streets. There's Roman Road, Roman Way and Hadrian Close, the latter commemorating the Roman Emperor who built Hadrian's Wall in the north of England. The old dock at Portus Abonae got a new lease of life in 1712 when Joshua Franklyn, a local merchant, founded a wet dock on the site. He believed it would save ships making the hazardous journey through the twisting and treacherous Avon Gorge with its fast-moving tide, to reach the wharves at Bristol.

Franklyn set up the Sea Mills Dock Company, which attracted thirty-two investors, but the enterprise was never a success. It turned out that the poor condition of the roads made it just as difficult to transport cargoes into Bristol. This meant that goods had to be taken up the River Avon by barge.

After Franklyn's attempt to turn the dock into a prosperous concern had failed, other merchants tried their hand but success eluded them, too. Sea Mills Dock was finally abandoned by the end of the eighteenth century, when it gradually fell into disrepair. However, remains of some of Joshua Franklyn's harbour walls can still be seen today.

In 1899, the foundations of an extensive villa were discovered by workmen building a new road at Brislington in the south-east of the city, and some mosaic pavements from the site have been preserved in Bristol Museum. It is thought that the villa, built around AD 270–300, was at the centre of a large Roman estate that had been destroyed by fire.

Remains of various Roman villas were often unearthed by builders developing new housing estates in the twentieth century. Builders constructing the Lawrence Weston suburb in 1947 discovered what has become known as the Kings Weston Roman Villa. The remains of the property, a Scheduled Ancient Monument, include a Roman bath suite, the only one that can be seen in Bristol, two third-century mosaic floors and the remains of a central heating system. Another settlement at Inns Court in the south of the city had possibly developed from earlier Iron Age farmsteads.

The *Western Daily Press* of 28 July 1972 reported that human bones were discovered in a 1,800-year-old stone coffin by an excavator driver working on a building site in Coombe Dingle in the Westbury on Trym district. Mike Ponsford, an archaeologist at Bristol Museum, told the paper's reporter that he thought the bones were those of a Romano-British woman of the second century. She was buried with a flagon in a 450lb Bath stone coffin, he said. 'The flagon probably contained wine as a gift to the gods in some after-life. I think she must have been a well-to-do woman, perhaps a farmer's wife,' said Mr Ponsford.

Older than Bristol

It seems to be little known that the suburb of Westbury on Trym is much older than Bristol. As long ago as the eighth century, a church dedicated to Saints Peter and Paul stood near the River Trym. Later there was a Benedictine monastery at Westbury and in 1194 Bishop Celestine set up a college of priests that existed for 300 years, making Westbury an important ecclesiastical centre. The earliest parts of the present Holy Trinity parish church date back to about 1200.

Westbury on Trym, 4 miles north of the centre of Bristol, has an ecclesiastical claim to fame in that reformer, theologian, priest and biblical translator John Wycliffe was made a prebendary of Westbury in the fourteenth century. He is better known, of course, for completing a translation of the Bible directly from the Vulgate into Middle English in 1382.

In close proximity to the church is a house believed to be one of the oldest domestic buildings in Bristol. The house in Church Road was the home of Elsie Briggs from 1958 until her death thirty years later. She left the house, which dates back to the fifteenth century, to trustees with instructions that it be kept as an ecumenical place of contemplative prayer.

The village itself has a literary association. Bristol-born Poet Laureate Robert Southey rented a house in Southfield Road for a year from 1798 when he wrote some of his poetry and articles for magazines.

The boundary of Bristol was extended in 1904 to take in Westbury on Trym. Since then it has developed from being a rural village to a bustling suburb.

WHAT'S IN A NAME?

Quite a lot it seems when it comes to that of Bristol. The town of Brycgstow – Old English meaning 'the place at the bridge' – was in existence by the start of the eleventh century. Through the years the spelling and pronunciation of Brycgstow has undergone many changes before becoming Bristol.

The name of Bristol has travelled far and wide, undoubtedly thanks to the explorers who set out from Bristol's tiny port in search of new lands. Many villages, towns and cities in the United States of America are named after the English town.

One of Bristol's oldest suburbs, Bedminster, has a township in New Jersey named after it. New Jersey is in the County of Somerset, which is quite apt for our own Bedminster was for many years a small town in the adjoining county of Somerset.

Not every overseas Bristol is in America. An arm of the Bering Sea is called Bristol Bay, as is an island in the Southern Atlantic Ocean. Quebec in Canada has a municipality called Bristol.

More than 200 hotels around the world are named Bristol but no one knows for certain why they have adopted the name. One obvious theory is that they are named after the English city. Another is that they take their name from Frederick Hervey, 4th Earl of Bristol and Bishop of Derry, Northern Ireland. He travelled widely, especially around Europe, and gained a reputation for only staying at the best hotels. Hence those he stayed at changed their names to Hotel Bristol. The title Marquis of Bristol has been held by a member of the Hervey family since 1714.

3

FROM THE SAXONS
TO THE NORMANS

An early mention of the town we now know as Bristol came as a passing reference in the *Anglo Saxon Chronicle* of 1051 to a place called Brycgstow. It was said to be a port with ships heading to and from Ireland. The earliest bridge would have spanned the river at the lowest feasible crossing point and would have been built of timber.

Most historians agree that it was near the present Bristol Bridge, probably east of it, that a settlement was founded on a peninsula almost encircled by the Rivers Avon and Frome and a moat. Archaeological excavations in the twentieth century suggest that this early settlement was formed in the Anglo-Saxon period on the site that is now Castle Park.

In 1247 the bridge was replaced by a new structure built on four stone arches. One of its features was the houses of four or five storeys in height on both sides that jutted out from the bridge over the River Avon. The houses had shop windows at ground-floor level and, perhaps unsurprisingly, their cellars were flooded from time to time.

Bristol Bridge was regarded as the place for the wealthy to live. At one time a community of goldsmiths lived and

Bristol Bridge, showing houses built above the arches

carried on their ancient trade here. The bridge was spanned in the middle by a high arch on which a chapel was built, facing east to west, with a priest's home attached. It must have been something of a grand sight, looking rather like London Bridge across the Thames.

In 1647 the bridge was struck by fire, with twenty-four of its timber houses being destroyed. To keep the repair bill low, stone and wood from the partly destroyed Raglan Castle in Wales were brought down the Rivers Wye and Severn on rafts to help rebuild the houses.

A close-up of Bristol Bridge

As the volume of traffic using Bristol Bridge grew, a larger crossing was built in 1768 at a cost of £49,000. The architect chosen for this job was aptly named James Bridges. The present structure is very much as Bridges left it, although there have since been improvements with footpaths being added on either side.

CROSSING THE 'CITY OF WATER'

Bristol is where it is thanks to the River Avon, also known as the Bristol Avon or the Lower Avon to distinguish it from other rivers elsewhere in the country bearing the same name. In the twelfth century, substantial amounts of wine from Bordeaux were shipped up the Avon into the centre of Bristol and ever since the river has played a pivotal part in the city's prosperity.

The Bristol Avon travels for 70 miles from its source at Acton Turville near Chipping Sodbury in Gloucestershire until it eventually merges with the River Severn at its estuary at Avonmouth after a tortuous journey. On its progress to Bristol, the Avon passes through the Wiltshire towns of Melksham and Bradford on Avon, before passing through Bath.

Another local river, the Frome, rises at Doddington in South Gloucestershire and wends its way through the villages of Iron Acton and Hambrook before reaching Stapleton when it enters Bristol. It joins the River Avon, now under the concrete of the city centre roads, and then heads towards the Avon Gorge and out to sea.

As Bristol grew, the Rivers Avon and Frome needed to be bridged to allow ships into the city docks, people to move around on foot easily and goods to be transported from the docks to Temple Meads railway station.

The Bristol Harbour Railway opened in 1872 to carry cargoes from the city docks to Temple Meads and vice versa. Its route included a tunnel under St Mary Redcliffe church. To cross Bathurst Basin to reach the docks, trains travelled across a steam-operated Bascule bridge. The Harbour Railway closed as a commercial operation in the 1960s. However, it is now a heritage railway running for about a mile along the south side of the docks.

Bristol, being relatively small in physical size, has more bridges than many a larger town. Down the centuries nearly fifty bascular bridges, footbridges and swing bridges of all shapes and sizes have been added to the city's infrastructure.

Wickham Bridge in Wickham Glen at Stapleton is believed to have been built in the early seventeenth century, although it may have replaced a medieval structure. The present crossing is a footbridge built on semicircular stone arches. It crosses the River Frome and is a Grade II listed building.

A close runner-up in terms of age is the Grade II listed Kingsweston iron bridge, built around 1800. It crosses the busy Kings Weston Road and is a link between the historic estates of Blaise Castle and Kings Weston House, the latter a mansion standing in vast grounds of its own in northwest Bristol.

Perhaps one of the most unusual bridges was the Ashton road and rail swing bridge. Built in 1906, it had two decks – one along the top for carrying a road and the other taking the Great Western Railway across the New Cut. The section of the bridge that could be swung was operated hydraulically from an overhead cabin. Thousands of people flocked to the bridge on its opening day so they could say they were among the first to walk over it. In recent years the bridge has been totally revamped and is now part of a guided busway and local access cycle path.

Apart from his spectacular Clifton Suspension Bridge, Isambard Kingdom Brunel built another bridge almost within the shadow of his masterpiece. It is identified by local people as BOB or 'Brunel's other bridge'. It was his first large rotating wrought iron opening bridge and carried road traffic over one of the locks at Cumberland Basin. It was built fifteen years before the suspension bridge and was decommissioned in the mid-1960s when the present Cumberland Basin flyover and swing bridge were completed. Since then it has been left to rust and rot on the dockside. It is listed Grade II* and is on English Heritage's Buildings at Risk Register. Engineering enthusiasts have been carrying out emergency repairs and development work on a voluntary basis, hoping that it can be restored as a river crossing.

One of the newest bridges twists its way over the Floating Harbour near the site of Bristol's old castle. The Castle Bridge cost nearly £3 million and is unusual in that it was made of curved steel sections. Canal barges were used to bring construction materials to the site. Specialist divers helped survey the site and prepare it for the underwater work. The footbridge, nearly 300ft long, was completed in 2017.

DOMESDAY BOOK

The Great Survey of 1086, which is better known as Domesday Book, listed 13,418 places, or settlements, in most of England and parts of Wales. Bristol was not given an individual entry. Instead it was described as being part of the royal manor of Barton Regis, which was then in the county of Gloucestershire. The name Barton still exists in the Barton Hill district. Barton Regis was listed as having thirty-nine households. The fact that those compiling Domesday Book had not included Bristol separately is not surprising. Also omitted from the book are Winchester, County Durham and Northumberland.

However, Domesday contained an entry for the Bristol suburb now known as Clifton but then called Clistone. Its name denoted a hillside settlement. Clistone was described as a village of 861 acres, inhabited by six villeins (tenant farmers) and their families, six bords (poultry farmers) and their dependants, along with three serfs (slave workers) as well as their children.

Clifton was in the County of Gloucestershire until 1835, when it was transferred through local government boundary changes into Bristol. At the same time, parts of what are now the suburb of Bedminster along with St Paul, St James, and St Philip and Jacob also came under the jurisdiction of Bristol, giving it a population of more than 110,000.

Domesday Book was commissioned in December 1085 by King William I almost two decades after the Norman Conquest of England. The King needed to raise taxes to pay for his army and so he set a survey in motion to assess the wealth and assets of his subjects. His commissioners travelled around the land covering forty counties to gather the information that the King wanted. So much information was gathered that Domesday Book ran to more than 900 pages of script containing 2 million words. It described the landholdings and resources of the population in the late eleventh century. The manuscript was written in medieval Latin and is now kept in the National Archives at Kew, London, in a specially made chest.

A list of Bristol businessmen, although it probably did not include everyone, was published by James Sketchley in his *Bristol Directory* in 1775. Among the merchants Sketchley included whip makers, sugar refiners, soap makers and snuff manufacturers who were exporting their goods.

IN THE MONEY

It was during the reign of the Saxon King Ethelred the Unready from 978 to 1016 that the first coins were minted in Bristol. The discovery of a silver penny bearing the inscription 'Aelfwere on Bric' – Bric being a contraction of Bristol – shows that by the tenth century Bristol was regarded as being important enough to have its own mint. At the time the law would only allow market towns to issue coins.

Coins were struck in Bristol on and off during the reigns of succeeding monarchs. When Edward I was on the throne (1272–1307) he gave orders that there should be four furnaces in Bristol and that homes for the men who worked in the mint should be provided in the castle. The last-known mint in the town was set up during the reign of William III (1696–97).

THE JEWS IN OLD BRISTOL

For a medieval religious relic, believed to be unique in this country, a building halfway along Jacob's Wells Road has been put to an unusual variety of uses in modern days. At one time it was used as a bicycle shed by constables at the police station on the opposite side of the road. It also served as a workshop for the restoration of antiques and at another time it became part of the local fire station.

Behind the walls of the curved, stone building is the only known medieval Mikveh, or Ritual Bath, in Britain used by the Jewish community. The history of the spring that feeds the Ritual Bath is believed to date back to about 1140 when there was a Jewish community living in Bristol. It is believed that Jacob's Well, as the spring became known, was used in burial ceremonies where bodies of deceased Jews were washed before interment. Close to the Ritual Bath was a Jewish burial ground, known as Jew's Acre, thought to have been set up in the eleventh century and probably the first cemetery of its kind in Bristol. A school now stands on the site. A stone lintel found inside the Mikveh bears an inscription in Hebrew, which is partly damaged but has been interpreted as meaning 'flowing water' or 'living water'.

The wholesale banishment of the Jewish community from England in 1290 led to many of their sacred sites becoming lost or forgotten. Under their laws Jews were forbidden from destroying religious artefacts, even if they were no longer used.

After the Jews had left England the spring passed to the Crown, which allowed monks from St Augustine's Abbey to use it when it was granted Scriptural Title. In 1373 King Edward III granted the spring to the people of Bristol by charter provided that a conduit was created to supply water to the town. After that, for hundreds of years the Ritual Bath seems to have disappeared from history. Its rediscovery in 1987 caused much local and national interest, especially among archaeologists.

The government declared the Ritual Bath to be a Scheduled Ancient Monument and English Heritage said it regarded Jacob's Well as potentially a monument of the highest importance both for the history of the Jewish community in England and for medieval studies generally.

Water from the well was last bottled in the 1980s when several businessmen set up separate enterprises to sell the spring water. These schemes were short-lived. Since then the building has been closed, with thousands of commuters passing by each day unaware of its religious importance.

A Castle Fit for Royalty

The first castle built in Bristol was a motte and bailey constructed of timber. It was later replaced by a stone-built castle, which the Normans started to construct about 1120. It was designed to guard the Saxon town then known as Bricgstow. With its great keep, or tower, the castle dominated the local landscape for 600 years. It stood on what is now open parkland in the centre of Bristol appropriately called Castle Park. The castle was built immediately east of St Peter's church, of which the bombed ruins still stand.

Robert Fitzroy, First Earl of Gloucester, half-brother to Queen Matilda and commander of her troops, built the

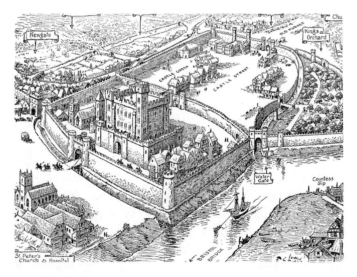

Bristol Castle

castle, thereby making what was said to be one of the strongest and safest stone fortresses in the land. The topographer William Worcester recorded that the castle's keep was 'twenty-five feet thick at the base, nine and a half feet at the eaves under the lead roofing and sixty foot in length east to west, and forty-five feet north to south'.

The castle had four towers with turrets, one at each of its corners, and was surrounded by water on three sides – the River Avon and the River Frome on two of them and a moat on the third. There were secret passages and subterranean dungeons. The castle was divided into two parts, an inner ward and an outer ward. The former contained the Chapel of St Martin, while the dungeons and living quarters for the garrison were in the outer ward. One of the castle's features was a banqueting hall, which was said to be 36 yards long and 18 yards wide with a marble dining table 15ft long. Only a few crumbling walls, underground chambers and the sally-port (tunnel) to the river remain of the original building.

Many a king made use of the banqueting hall when he was in Bristol for meetings with local gentry, entertaining the town's dignitaries, or simply to relax after a day's hunting in the King's Wood.

Edward II was once a prisoner here before meeting his death in Berkeley Castle. In 1141 King Stephen was imprisoned in Bristol Castle after being captured during his attempt to claim the English throne. Princess Eleanor of Brittany, known as the Beauty of Brittany, was held prisoner from 1202 until her death forty years later. Imprisoned by King John, she was guarded by four knights in case she had the opportunity of engaging in a clandestine marriage by which the succession of the crown might become disputable. After her death, Princess Eleanor was at first buried in the churchyard of the nearby St James Priory but her remains were later exhumed and reinterred at a nunnery at Amesbury near Salisbury, of which she had been a benefactor. It seems that Princess Eleanor was not treated inhumanely during her imprisonment, for she was allowed her own maids and limited freedom.

King John is said to have tortured wealthy Jewish businessmen in the castle if they resisted his demands for money.

Oliver Cromwell, Lord Protector, became Lord High Steward of the castle in 1651, by which time it was in the ownership of Bristol Corporation. In 1665 Cromwell ordered the corporation 'to dismantle and demolish' it. Apparently, the building was in a state of dereliction. Householders in the city were ordered to spend a day a week to level off the site. Some of the rubble from the castle was used in the construction of houses and roads that were later built on the site. Was this an early form of recycling?

Bristol Castle may not have left its mark in any big way on the history of England but it did at least get a touch of theatrical fame. It gets a mention – albeit a rather fleeting one – in one of Shakespeare's plays. It can be found in Act 2 Scene 3 of *Richard II*.

NORMANDY IN BRISTOL

St James Priory in the Horsefair claims the distinction of being not only the city's oldest place of worship but also its oldest building. It is also a legacy of Norman architecture. Standing next to a bus station built in the 1960s, one couldn't ask for a more striking contrast in architectural styles.

It is said that when Robert, First Earl of Gloucester and son of King Henry I, was building Bristol Castle with stone brought from Caen, Normandy, he devoted every tenth stone to the construction of St James Priory. This was to serve as a Benedictine cell of Tewkesbury Abbey.

It included a refectory, chapter house, dormitory, cloister, farm buildings, cemetery, gardens and a gatehouse. The church was consecrated in 1129 by Simon, Bishop of Worcester.

During the Reformation all the buildings of the priory, except the parish church, were destroyed on the orders of Henry VIII. As distinct from a monastery, the priory church had been designed to serve both monks and parishioners. The priory was also the centre of social welfare in medieval Bristol with monks offering help to people in need.

After the Reformation, St James church became part of the Church of England but since 1966 it has been an active church within the Roman Catholic Diocese of Clifton. It is still open to the public.

St James contains more remains of Norman architecture, including pillars and arches in the nave, than any other church building in Bristol. Its west front has a rose window in the gable that is thought to be the oldest such window in the country.

In the eighteenth century John Wesley and his brother Charles, founders of the Methodist Church, considered this as their local parish church when they were in Bristol. The brothers often worshipped and preached at St James and some of Charles Wesley's children, including Samuel who became a distinguished composer and organist, were baptised in the church.

The builders of Norman churches certainly didn't do things by half. Take, for example, St Augustine's Abbey, which was is said to be the wealthiest of Bristol's monastic houses. It was founded in 1140 by Robert Fitzharding, a wealthy and prominent Bristol citizen who later became Lord Berkeley of Gloucestershire. St Augustine's Abbey was a large monastic complex built on a terrace of rock immediately above Canon's Marsh. Its lands stretched in one direction uphill to Brandon Hill Park and in the opposite it took in much of the area known today as the city centre. A school has stood on the abbey site since the twelfth century, making Bristol Cathedral Choir School the oldest educational establishment in the city.

Robert Fitzharding imported the abbey's first six monks from a monastery in Herefordshire. They were known as Black Canons on account of the long black cloaks with black hoods they wore.

St Augustine's Abbey, which later became Bristol Cathedral, was dedicated on Easter Day 1148 at a special service attended by various church dignitaries including the Bishops of Exeter, Llandaff, St Asaph and Worcester, Bristol being part of the latter diocese at the time. Fitzharding later became a canon in his own abbey and was buried there.

The Norman remains of the abbey can still be seen in the cathedral's chapter house, the abbey gatehouse and the buildings occupied by the school.

4

CREATING A CITY
AND COUNTY

Bristol has had a Mayor since 1216 when Roger Cordewaner – his name comes from his trade as a shoemaker – held the post. Since then there has been an unbroken list of holders of the office. In 1899 Queen Victoria granted Bristol the privilege of calling its Mayor, or First Citizen, the Right Honourable Lord Mayor of Bristol. A new Lord Mayor takes up his or her duties on Mayor Making Day each May, having been elected by fellow members of the city council. The name of every First Citizen from 1216 onwards is engraved on a wall in the conference room of the City Hall.

An unusual instance of the exercise of an ancient mayoral right occurred in 1792 when John Noble was the Mayor. When he was in London Mr Noble made his way to the Court of Admiralty at Westminster while it was in session. He claimed a right to preside in company with the judge. Needless to say, the judge was taken aback and about to have Mayor Noble ejected from the court room when he produced a charter of Edward IV. This confirmed the privilege of the Mayor of Bristol to take his seat on the bench of any law court in the land. Having made his point, Mr Noble withdrew from the court immediately.

Local authorities are not generally regarded as being in the vanguard of change. Bristol had to wait more than 700 years before it had its first woman Lord Mayor. In 1963 Florence Brown, who had been elected to the city council in 1937 and became an alderman eighteen years later, was chosen by her colleagues for the post. Women Lord Mayors are now commonplace in Bristol.

The Lord Mayor's official regalia dates from medieval times and comprises a scarlet robe edged in fur, a feathered tricorn hat, gauntlets and a gold chain of office, which alone weighs nearly 3lb. On occasion the Lord Mayor is expected to wear velvets and a dress sword. This has long been the correct outfit for men of distinction appearing at court.

THE LORD MAYOR'S OWN CHAPEL

Bristol City Council has the distinction of being the only local authority in the country to own and maintain a church or chapel. Although it is formally dedicated to St Mark, this place of worship is popularly known as the Lord Mayor's Chapel. It does not have a parish.

The chapel was created in 1220 by Maurice de Gaunt, the grandson of Robert Fitzharding, the founder of St Augustine's Abbey, which evolved into Bristol Cathedral. It was part of the Hospital of the Gaunts, which looked after the sick, fed the poor and provided schooling for twelve poor boys. Wealthy merchants of Bristol endowed the hospital with various manors in Gloucestershire, Somerset and Wiltshire as well as the land immediately surrounding the chapel.

Two years after the Hospital of the Gaunts was dissolved by Henry VIII in his suppression of the monasteries, Bristol Corporation bought the chapel and all its lands from the

Crown for £1,000. Ever since then St Mark's Chapel has been under the control of the local authority.

Later, the Mayor and Corporation of Bristol offered French Huguenots, who had left their homeland, use of the chapel. The Huguenots worshipped here until 1722. From then on the Mayor and other civic dignitaries attended divine service at the chapel. They had previously worshipped at Bristol Cathedral on the opposite side of College Green. However, after an unusual dispute with the Dean and Chapter, they decided to use St Mark's; after all it was their own church.

The dispute apparently centred on the city fathers, who were in the habit of leaving services before hearing the sermon, which in those days could last for an hour or more. In leaving the cathedral service early, council officials not only snubbed the preacher but were also said to have caused a commotion and upset the rest of the congregation.

For many years High Court judges, robed in red and bewigged, arrived by horse-drawn carriage for worship at the Lord Mayor's Chapel before going on to dispense justice at Bristol Assizes. This was a colourful tradition that fell by the wayside in 1974 when the assizes were abolished to be replaced by the Crown Court.

The chapel has some interior fixtures not normally seen in a church. Near the Mayor's seat is the rest for Bristol's State Sword. Brass brackets on each side of the rest hold the silver mace, which police constables carry as they process in front of the Mayor on state visits. There is also a special place where the City Sword Bearer can place his or her Cap of Maintenance during a service.

THE BLACK DEATH

Bristol's growing population received a big setback when the Black Death, or plague, arrived in the city in 1348. It is thought that the plague first surfaced in this country through a port in Dorset. It had probably been brought into the country by a sailor arriving from the Continent.

Bristol, with an estimated population of 10,000 at the time, was one of the first major English towns to be overwhelmed by the plague. One writer said that 'the plague raged to such a degree that the living were scarce able to bury their dead ... the grass grew several inches high in High Street and Broad Street. The parson of Holy Cross church had to extend his cemetery by half an acre because so many people in the district had died.' The parson, however, did this without first obtaining a royal licence to do so and subsequently had to beg for the King's pardon.

Describing the effect the plague had on Bristol, a monk by the name of Henry Knighton wrote in his *Latin Chronicle*, 'There died, suddenly overwhelmed by death, almost the whole strength of the town, for few were sick more than three days, or two days, or even half a day. Then this cruel death spread everywhere, following the course of the sun.'

The situation was so bad that the authorities in Gloucester gave orders that no travellers from Bristol should enter their town.

The actual number of deaths in Bristol caused by the plague is unknown but it is believed that between 30 and 40 per cent of the population lost their lives. This slowed Bristol's growth and caused the community to remain between 10,000 and 12,000 through to the sixteenth century before it started picking up again. The Black Death subsided towards the end of 1349 and it is estimated that between 40 and 60 per cent of England's population was wiped out by it.

BRISTOL'S VERY OWN MAGNA CARTA

During Bristol's early years one of its principal events was the granting of a charter by King Edward III in 1373. Its official title was 'The Charter of Liberties', although it became affectionately known as Bristol's own Magna Carta.

As far as the citizens were concerned, this was no ordinary charter for it raised the town from borough status to that of an independent county in its own right. Bristol was the first provincial borough outside of London to be elevated to such status.

The charter stated that the new county of Bristol would be completely separate from the counties of Gloucester and Somerset. Until this time Bristol was divided, geographically and administratively, by the River Avon. The parishes to the west and north of the river were in Gloucestershire while those to the south were in Somerset.

In the charter, dated 8 August 1373, the King stated that from 'henceforth Bristol shall be separate from the counties of Gloucester and Somerset equally and in all things exempt, as well by land as by water, and that it shall be a county by itself and be called the County of Bristol forever ...'

The charter was a reward for Bristol's naval patriotism in providing the King with twenty-three ships and 608 men at the siege of Calais. This was only two ships and fifty-four men fewer than London. Money also changed hands for the charter with Bristol giving the King 600 marks, for which he would have been extremely grateful as it enabled him to continue the Hundred Years' War against France.

As a result of the charter, Bristol could now send two members to Parliament and elect forty 'of the better and more honest people' to form a council that had the powers to levy rates and taxes. The charter also gave Bristol the privilege of appointing a sheriff.

An official residence and office is provided for the Lord Mayor during his or her term of office. The Mansion House, with its twenty-two rooms on the edge of Clifton Down, was given to the city by its developer and first occupant, Alderman Thomas Proctor in 1874 on his wedding anniversary. Such a generous gift came as a surprise to the city fathers, who were further taken aback to discover the house came complete with fixtures and furnishings. Mr Proctor also threw in a cheque for £500 to help cover the cost of any repairs and decorations that might be needed. The house replaced the original Mansion House in Queen Square, which was destroyed in the Bristol Reform Riots of 1831.

Many of Bristol's civic traditions and ceremonies date back to the time of the King's charter. The Mayor was given the right to have a sword carried in front of him on all civic occasions, hence the creation of the office of City Swordbearer, which still exists. The Swordbearer is the only person allowed to wear a head-covering – a furry Cossack-type of cap known as the Cap of Maintenance – in the presence of royalty. The cap and sword symbolise inflexible justice and the Mayor's right and readiness to defend the interest of the burgesses, or citizens, whenever necessary.

The charter gave Bristol new courts including Courts of Assize and of Quarter Sessions. It meant that towns-folk with business in the courts would no longer have to make the long and costly journey to the assize towns of Gloucester or Ilchester in Somerset. They would now be able to conduct their legal affairs in Bristol.

The sea boundaries of the new county extended to the islands of Flat Holm and Steep Holm in the Bristol Channel, which lie between Weston-super-Mare and Cardiff, a distance of 25 miles from the centre of Bristol itself. The sea boundary of Bristol skirts around Clevedon Pier and includes the lighthouse on Battery Point at Portishead. It then returns to dry land via tiny Denny Island, for Avonmouth, from where the river boundary goes to Chittening Warth, in the north, and then on under the Clifton Suspension Bridge and to its most northerly point at Hanham Weir. This boundary has remained virtually unchanged since 1373.

Another charter granted by King Edward III gave Bristol the right to arrest people who disturbed the peace at night. Bakers who sold bread under an agreed weight would also face a penalty. This was a way of controlling the price of bread and avoiding public disorder when grain was scarce and expensive.

CROSS MARKS THE SPOT

Being granted the Charter of Liberties prompted the city fathers to mark the momentous occasion by building a permanent monument in the centre of town. The High Cross, as it was known, was erected at the crossroads of the four main streets of old Bristol – Wine Street, Corn Street, Broad Street and High Street.

By all accounts the High Cross was a rather grand affair. Celia Fiennes, a travel writer who visited every county in England on horseback, passed through Bristol in 1698 and described it as 'a very high and magnificent Cross built all of stone or sort of marble of the country'. She described it as being 'adorned with figures of beasts and birds and flowers'.

The High Cross

Originally the High Cross had four niches in which were installed statues of four Plantagenet kings. In 1633 the cross was heightened and four more statues added depicting Henry VI, Elizabeth I, James I and Charles I. The monument was now just shy of 40ft high. Apparently it was brightly painted and gilded and protected by an iron palisade.

Not only was the High Cross a landmark but it was also the location for civic proclamations and a place where councillors assembled for processions. News of accessions to the throne were always announced here, as was Henry VIII's decision that he had made Bristol a bishopric in 1542.

The High Cross was taken down when John Vaughan, a wealthy banker living nearby, claimed that his life and property were in danger when it started shaking in high winds. It was removed to College Green alongside Bristol Cathedral. However, it wasn't long before more complaints were made. This time a number of people objected to the siting of the cross, which they said prevented them from promenading – a craze at the time of people walking up to ten abreast. The High Cross was taken down again and this time stored in bits in the cloisters of the cathedral.

The last that the citizens of Bristol saw of their monument was when six horse-drawn wagons, each bearing various parts of the High Cross, left the cathedral to be taken to Wiltshire. Apparently, the Dean of Bristol, Dr Cutts Barton, had made a gift of it to his friend Henry Hoare, a collector of antiques, who installed it on his estate at Stourhead Park. It has stood there since 1768 and is maintained by the National Trust, which now owns Stourhead Park.

However, the saga of the High Cross was not over in Bristol by any means. A replica of it was commissioned and installed on College Green, where it stayed until 1950 when the land was lowered. Somehow, the replica found its way into a builder's yard, where it was left to crumble. A public appeal was set up by local conservation groups to restore the monument, part of which now stands in a corner of a communal garden in Berkeley Square, Clifton. Very few people, though, seem to be aware of its existence – or if they do know, they are unaware of what it represents.

Another view of the High Cross

THE PARK WITH TALES TO TELL

Apart from being a temporary home for the High Cross, College Green is one of the most historic sites in the centre of the city. This green space of nearly 3 acres with Bristol

Cathedral on one side and the Lord Mayor's Chapel on the other takes the shape of a segment of a circle.

At one time an open-air pulpit stood here. In the middle of the park was a chapel dedicated to St Jordan, a follower of St Augustine of Canterbury. Monks from St Augustine's Abbey also used College Green as their burial ground.

After the Dissolution of the Monasteries the site became known as Bishop's Park. Presumably, this was on account of its ownership, along with that of the remains of St Augustine's Abbey, being transferred to the Dean and Chapter of Bristol Cathedral. The park was later renamed College Green.

The cathedral authorities still own this slice of open parkland. However, the city council is responsible for its maintenance through legal documents issued by the Dean and Chapter of the cathedral in 1894.

In one corner of the park stands a marble statue of Queen Victoria erected by the people of Bristol at a cost of £1,500 in 1887 to commemorate Her Majesty's Golden Jubilee. The sculptor Joseph Boehm, who was often commissioned by the royal family and members of the aristocracy to make sculptures for their parks and gardens, made the statue. He has depicted the Queen holding an orb and sceptre. The statue, which weighs 4 tons, was made from one block of white marble and stands on a circular pedestal. It was unveiled by Queen Victoria's grandson, Prince Albert Victor, Duke of Clarence and Avondale, on 25 July 1888, a year after her jubilee.

Overlooking College Green are the headquarters of Bristol City Council. Its foundation stone was laid before the Second World War but construction work was interrupted by the hostilities and the national economic situation that followed. The curved offices, replacing a much older building in Corn Street, were opened by Queen Elizabeth II in 1956 when she made her first official visit to the city as

Queen. The building was officially known as the Council House until 2012, when it was changed to City Hall by Bristol's first directly elected Mayor.

HOW BRISTOL GOT ITS CATHEDRAL

King Henry VIII, who ascended to the throne in 1509, turned out to be one of the most famous monarchs in English history. This was not only for having six wives but also for breaking away from the Roman church and appointing himself as Supreme Head of the Church of England.

Breaking away from the Papacy meant that Henry VIII dissolved all convents and monasteries and confiscated their revenues and any land they held. In Bristol this included the suppression of St Augustine's Abbey on College Green. By the time of the Dissolution the monks had enlarged their original abbey, adding the north transept and central tower. The nave was also being rebuilt but the work had not been completed.

Three years after the Dissolution, the King created six Church of England dioceses, including one for Bristol, and gave the city its cathedral. This was built from the remains of St Augustine's Abbey and formally became the Cathedral Church of the Holy and Undivided Trinity. It was also the seat of the newly created Bishop of Bristol. For this post King Henry appointed one of his chaplains, the Reverend Paul Bush. Befitting an ecclesiastical pioneer, Bishop Bush, who died in 1558, has an ornate tomb in the cathedral's Eastern Lady Chapel. His wife, who died five years earlier than him, is buried nearby.

The name of the Diocese of Bristol today is something of a misnomer. Not only does the diocese cover Bristol, but stretches from Avonmouth in the west to the Wiltshire town of Swindon in the east and takes in parts of South Gloucestershire.

For more than 300 years until the middle of the nineteenth century the new cathedral was without a nave, the original having been demolished because of its dangerous state. The only space for worship was a shut-off partition of the choir with room for just several hundred worshippers. Minor canons at the cathedral were excused attendance at early morning prayers from the beginning of November 1761 to the end of the following March after complaining that the cold building was 'very dangerous and detrimental to their health'.

The nave was completed to its medieval design, and built on the old foundations in 1868. Two towers were later added to the west end. The cathedral's architecture is particularly special, being one of the finest examples of a medieval 'hall church': the vaulted ceilings of its nave, choir and aisles are all of the same height. Bristol Cathedral is a mixture of many architectural styles including Norman, Early English, Early Decorated, Decorated and Perpendicular.

Bristol Cathedral made ecclesiastical history in 1994 when the ordination of the first women into the Church of England priesthood took place there. This was the culmination of the most bitterly fought battle within the church since Henry VIII's Reformation. There was both support and opposition to this move by churchmen and women from all parts of the Anglican Communion. At the precise time of the Ordination Service one Church of England vicar tolled the funeral bell at his church, not far from Bristol Cathedral. During the service a team of vergers equipped with 'walkie-talkie' radios patrolled the packed cathedral looking for potential troublemakers. In the event there were no problems.

In the service the Rev. Angela Berners-Wilson had the honour of being the first woman to be ordained when the

The Pro-Cathedral in Park Place. It is now residential accommodation.

then Bishop of Bristol, the Rt Rev. Barry Rogerson, laid his hands on her head. Altogether thirty-two women were ordained during the service, which was broadcast by television and radio around the world and put Bristol Cathedral firmly on the global stage.

Besides the Anglican cathedral Bristol also has a Roman Catholic cathedral dedicated to Saints Peter and Paul. The cathedral in Clifton was consecrated in 1973. It was constructed in three years, making it the fastest-built cathedral in Britain since the Middle Ages. At the consecration service Cardinal Heenan described the cathedral as 'the ecclesiastical bargain of the century', referring to its cost of £600,000. It replaced the Pro-Cathedral, which had been built in Park Place, Clifton, in 1848 as the Church of the Twelve Apostles. It became the Pro-Cathedral, acting in place of a cathedral, two years later when Clifton was created an Episcopal See.

Clifton Cathedral is the 'Mother Church' for Roman Catholics not only in Bristol but also in the counties of Gloucestershire, Somerset, and Wiltshire.

A COAT OF ARMS FOR BRISTOL

Bristol was officially granted its Coat of Arms in 1569. It was based on seals that are believed to have been first used in the charter that Edward III granted to Bristol in 1373. The Coat of Arms depicts a ship leaving the watergate of a castle with two towers, which indicates a strongly fortified port. On each side of the crest is a golden unicorn and underneath is Bristol's motto, 'Virtute et Industria', which translated from the Latin means virtue and industry.

A Coat of Arms, crests, badges and supporters can only be granted by letters patent issued by the most senior heralds, the Kings of Arms. These officers with such imposing titles act according to powers delegated to them by the Crown and all grants are therefore made under Crown authority. Bristol's Coat of Arms can be seen on many buildings and bridges throughout the city.

The gilded unicorns that stand at each end of the roof of the City Hall (formerly the Council House) on College Green took council officers by surprise when they were installed in 1950 as they had not been included in the original plans for the building.

However, they were ordered later and put in place at the request of the city architect. He explained to the councillors that the 12ft-high unicorns cost £2,400, whereas ornamental ridging along the length of the roof would have been more expensive.

5

SHIPSHAPE AND BRISTOL FASHION

The story of Bristol is inseparable from the story of the sea. There has been a port in the Bristol area since Roman times and maritime trade has been a key part of the city's life ever since.

The port being situated right in the middle of town attracted some of the country's best-known writers and poets to eulogise about it. In the early part of the twelfth century, the monk and historian William of Malmesbury described it as 'a port which is a commodious and safe harbour for all vessels, into which come ships from Ireland and Norway and from other lands beyond the seas.'

Putting pen to paper in 1739, the poet and satirist Alexander Pope wrote about the docks, saying that:

> In the middle of the street, as far as you can see, hundreds of ships, their masts as thick as they can stand by one another, which is the oddest and most surprising sight imaginable. The street is fuller of them than the Thames from London Bridge to Deptford.

Part of the City Docks with Bristol Bridge in the background after
the houses were removed

Daniel Defoe, best known for his novel *Robinson Crusoe*,
wrote in another of his books, *Tour Through the Whole
Island of Great Britain*, 'The greatest, the richest and the
best port of trade in Great Britain, London only excepted.'

The writer H. V. Morton in his book *In Search of England*,
published in 1927, wrote:

> Ships come right into Bristol town ... and the men of Bristol
> think nothing of it. They have been accustomed to this dis-
> turbing sight for over nine centuries. It must occur to a man
> looking at Bristol for the first time that a city that welcomes
> ships to her bosom in this manner could not help carving a
> great future on the seas.

Thirteenth-Century Port Expansion

By the thirteenth century, Bristol had become a busy port. Wine from Bordeaux had been the principal import since the twelfth century, while exports included woollen cloth, iron and lead.

As trade expanded it was realised that more space for berthing ships was needed. Work started in 1241 on diverting the course of the River Frome by taking it through marshland that was owned by St Augustine's Abbey but had been granted to the Corporation of Bristol. Excavating a trench 2,400ft long, 18ft deep and 120ft wide to divert the River Frome was a mammoth task. It took workmen using their hands, spades and shovels, seven years to complete.

Cargoes Galore

Some of the ships leaving Bristol were carrying cargoes to France, Spain, Ireland, Portugal and North Africa's Barbary Coast.

From the eighteenth century almost all the tobacco used by the Wills tobacco factories in the city was shipped into Bristol. In the 1970s the firm's daily payment of tobacco duty to HM Customs and Excise was about £850,000. Wills, in its heyday, was employing more than 6,000 local people. At one time the firm was producing more than 350 million cigarettes every week. Statistics like these make it hard to believe that tobacco was once a banned import in Bristol. London had a monopoly of the trade until 1639, when the Privy Council revoked a long-standing order that tobacco should only be shipped into the capital.

In the 1970s the council reported that the city docks were losing some £200,000 a year. A major revolution was taking place in the shipping industry worldwide as giant container ships were becoming the order of the day. Container ships were so big they were unable to negotiate the Avon Gorge to reach Bristol's docks. As a result, the council closed the city docks to commercial shipping. It meant the eventual demolition of landmark buildings such as the bonded tobacco warehouses at Canons Marsh.

The closure of the docks also meant that the last commercial vessel to be launched from Charles Hill's Albion shipyard took place in 1976. This was a tanker for the Guinness Brewery in Dublin. The Hill family and their forerunner Hillhouse had been building ships on the same site for more than 250 years. Hill's order book showed that their 3,644-tonne coastal oil tanker Anglo launched in 1959 was the biggest vessel ever built in Bristol.

Bristol's maritime history continues to grow with modern commercial shipping taking place 7 miles downriver at Avonmouth Docks and at the more modern Royal Portbury Dock officially opened by the Queen in 1977. Since 1991, Royal Portbury has been run by the Bristol Port Company, which bought a 150-year lease from the city council. Until then the Port of Bristol had the distinction of being the only major seaport in the United Kingdom under local authority control. Royal Portbury has become a major centre in the United Kingdom for the importation of motor vehicles.

Meanwhile, a maritime phrase coined in Bristol lives on in every-day speech. 'All shipshape and Bristol fashion' means that everything has been stowed and the ship is ready to go to sea. It is believed to derive from the port's reputation for efficiency in the days of sail.

The clock tower at Charles Hill's Albion Dockyard

DIGGING THE NEW CUT

At five o'clock on the first morning of May in 1804 work started on what must have been one of the largest civil engineering jobs at the time in Bristol, if not in the world. The first shovels of earth were dug to create the Floating Harbour.

Construction of the Floating Harbour involved impounding the tidal River Avon to enable ships to stay afloat all the time they were berthed in the docks instead of being stranded in mud when the tide receded. The Floating Harbour comprises about 2½ miles of waterway at an artificially maintained level.

The dock authorities decided that such a scheme was essential if the port was to expand, take bigger ships and provide a quicker turnaround for cargo handling. The city's prosperity was being threatened as merchants started to use other ports that were closer to the sea and more efficient.

William Jessop, who had started work on canal construction when he was just 16 years old, was commissioned to build the Floating Harbour. His work all over the country had put him in the top league of civil engineers. He took on his son to supervise this huge project.

An Act of Parliament was needed to divert a 2-mile-long stretch of the River Avon from Cumberland Basin to Totterdown. One thousand men were employed on digging and blasting what was to become known as the New Cut. The tools they used were mainly shovels, spades, picks, wheelbarrows and sheer muscle. Excavators and other mechanical aids were yet to be invented. Gunpowder was used to blast through the rock. Much of the hard sandstone was used to build the walls of the locks that were needed at Cumberland Basin as part of the scheme. The estimated cost of the whole project was £300,000 but at the end of the day the bill had risen to more than twice that figure.

Exactly five years to the day after work started on the New Cut, Jessop's scheme was completed. To celebrate the occasion, an open-air party was laid on for the workmen. One local newspaper reported that two whole oxen, 600cwt of plum pudding, potatoes and beef were included on the menu. For each man there was a gallon of beer. Perhaps unsurprisingly, with that amount of alcohol being consumed, a brawl broke out between English and Irish workmen.

In its early days the tidal New Cut was used by passenger steam packets sailing to South Wales and Ireland from a jetty that had been constructed at Bathurst Basin. No vessels, however, have used this waterway for many years, certainly not in living memory.

A TOAST TO THE WINE TRADE

In medieval times, wine imports to Bristol, mainly from France and Spain, accounted for almost a third of all the cargoes that arrived in the country. By the start of the fourteenth century, 250 gallons of wine a year arrived in Bristol from Bordeaux alone. A trades directory published towards the end of the nineteenth century listed no fewer than twenty-seven wine merchants in the city, not to be confused with the many retailers.

J.R. Phillips was once the oldest wine merchant in the city, being founded in 1739 by William George. The firm built up a successful selling line – Old English Cordials, which were originally produced as medication and for the prevention of illness on long sea voyages. Their cordials included lime juice (for the prevention of scurvy), celery-flavoured lovage (for rheumatism) and shrub, a potent mixture of juices and alcohol that was advertised as keeping colds at bay.

At one time the firm used the cellars beneath the Colston Hall – thought to be some of the oldest in the city and once used by monks – to keep its wine. The firm closed its depot in Avonmouth in 1991.

The name of Harveys Sherry became synonymous with that of Bristol. Founded in 1796 as a small family firm

The City Docks looking toward St Mary Redcliffe church

selling mainly Spanish and Portuguese wines, including port and sherry, in the nineteenth century, John Harvey created a new blend of sherry that was called Harveys Bristol Cream. It was blended in the firm's cellars in Denmark Street close to the city docks. As part of its publicity material, Harveys often related the story about a lady who was sampling the different sherries when she was offered Bristol Milk and afterwards another finer blend. 'If this is Bristol Milk,' she said, 'then this must be Bristol Cream.' In the 1960s

Harveys was exporting its sherry to 120 countries. The last Bristol Cream sherry to be bottled in the city was in 1989.

When the diarist Samuel Pepys visited Bristol he noted the absence of carts for carrying goods. Bristol Council had barred them from the city to prevent heavy loads from crushing the vaults beneath the streets, especially those where wine was stored. Goods had to be dragged along the streets on sledges.

ADVENTUROUS VENTURERS

One of the early roles of the Society of Merchant Venturers was to regulate all trade with the city to ensure that outsiders did not benefit at the expense of the people of Bristol. From early in the seventeenth century for about 200 years they managed Bristol's port. This included building and improving quays, putting in new cranes and maintaining towpaths. In return for these privileges the Merchants kept the River Avon clear of mud and fallen rocks from the gorge.

The organisation financed voyages of exploration and trading and became involved with the slavery and tobacco trades on the Bristol–Africa–America route. The Society had petitioned Parliament against the monopoly held by the Royal African Company in the slave trade. This led to the ending of the monopoly four years later and individual Society members were to be directly involved in the trade.

The Society of Merchant Venturers is one of the city's most historic organisations. It was officially established in 1552, when Edward VI granted the Society its first Royal Charter. However, it is thought that the Society dates back to a local guild of merchants founded in the thirteenth century.

The Merchant Venturers played a significant role in the construction of the Clifton Suspension Bridge and many of its members were directly involved in the building of the Great Western Railway. Increasingly, the Merchant Venturers have concentrated upon the Society's charitable concerns as a trustee of a number of organisations associated with Bristol including schools and homes for the elderly.

A number of Royal Charters or Letters Patent have been granted to the Society, including one from Elizabeth I which gave certain privileges as to the hours at which goods might be loaded and unloaded in the port. The present constitution of the Society is set out by a Royal Charter that stipulates an annual election takes place each November to find members for its Court, or executive body. The elections take place after members, wearing top hats and tails, have attended their annual service in Bristol Cathedral. In 1989 Elizabeth II increased the size of the Society's Court to fifteen members by way of a charter. The Society made history at its annual meeting in November 2020 when Gillian Camm was appointed the first female Master in its 468 years.

Membership of the Society now stands at seventy men and women, all of whom are members by invitation. Around eighty honorary members have been appointed during the Society's long history. One of the first was Major General Thomas Harrison, a Parliamentarian who had signed the death warrant of King Charles I. The first member of the royal family to become an Honorary Member was Prince Frederick of Wales in 1738. He has been followed in later years by the Duke of York in 1762, George, Prince of Wales in 1807, the Duke of Edinburgh in 1953 and Prince Charles in 1973. Princess Anne, the Princess Royal, received honorary membership in 2012.

The Society's Master at the time, David Marsh, said that Princess Anne's 'extensive charitable work and her commitment to enhancing the lives of those less fortunate' were very much in keeping with the Society's own values. The United Kingdom's first woman Prime Minister, Margaret Thatcher, and the former Archbishop of Canterbury, George Carey, now Lord Carey of Clifton, are also on the List of Honorary Members.

LAND AHOY!

Bristol being sited on the western side of England meant it was favourably situated as a launch pad for explorers, especially those seeking the 'new' lands we now know as North America.

Giovanni Caboto, better known by his Anglicised name of John Cabot, became the most famous explorer of all to sail from the city. Cabot, a Venetian, was the first European since the Vikings to land on mainland North America – not by intention though. He had set out to discover a trading route to find the silks and spices of the Orient. When Cabot and his son, Sebastian, with a crew of eighteen local men, left Bristol on 2 May 1497 in his caravel *The Matthew* they could hardly have envisaged that they were on their way to making maritime history.

The intrepid crew guided just by the stars – charts, compasses, two-way radio and radar were tools of the future – made landfall on 24 June. Cabot set foot, not on the soil of China or Japan, but somewhere in the New World. It's unclear where the exact spot was but historians generally accept it to be Newfoundland. No one knows for certain the exact route or any problems that Cabot's 50-ton square-rigged ship may have encountered crossing the Atlantic Ocean. Any log books or documents that Cabot may have kept have never been found.

Cabot's crew was back in Bristol on 6 August to be greeted by the mayor and corporation, representatives of many of the trade guilds along with a large gathering of citizens. The bells of eighteen city churches pealed a welcome. Cabot returned with a large whale bone, which ever since has been on display at St Mary Redcliffe church. Medieval explorers began and ended their voyages at the shrine of Our Lady of Redcliffe. Initially they prayed for a safe journey and on their return gave thanks for a trouble-free trip. They often came back with gifts for the church.

To make his epic voyage, Cabot was granted Letters Patent from King Henry VII to explore easier trading routes to Asia. In part the Letters Patent stated that he had been given '… full and free authority, leave and power to sail to all parts, countries and seas of the east, of the west and of the north to seek out, discover and find whatever isles, countries, regions or provinces … which before this time have been unknown to all Christians'. King Henry's document said that Cabot should 'set up our banners and ensigns in all such newly discovered lands and subdue, occupy and possess all such in the King's name'.

When Cabot reported to the King about his discovery he was awarded an annual pension of £20. This was paid out of the monies received for taxing goods arriving in Bristol's port. The port's senior Collector of Customs, Richard Ameryke, was responsible for handing over the pension. It has long been thought by many people in Bristol that the continent of North America was named after Ameryke, and not after another explorer, Amerigo Vespucci, as is generally believed.

John Cabot set sail from Bristol again in 1498 but it is believed that he died at sea. Bristolians have always taken pride in Cabot's voyage. To mark the 400th anniversary a 105ft-high tower, complete with viewing balcony at the top, was built on Brandon Hill. Cabot Tower, paid for by subscriptions from the citizens, was officially opened at a ceremony attended by distinguished guests from Bristol and Newfoundland.

Among other Bristol explorers were Martin Pring, who in 1603 at the age of 23 was the captain of an expedition to North America aimed at assessing commercial potential. He made landfall at the harbour where seventeen years later the Pilgrim Fathers landed. Pring explored areas of present-day Maine, New Hampshire and Cape Cod in Massachusetts. He discovered several rivers and returned home with medicinal plants including sassafras.

John Guy, a prominent Bristolian, became the first Governor General of Newfoundland. He had sailed with about forty people to set up the new colony. Guy's settlers took with them cattle, goats, poultry and rabbits, hoping they would settle in.

Guy partly funded the expedition himself with financial help from the Society of Merchant Venturers. He later served as Sheriff and Mayor of Bristol and was elected Master of the Venturers Society. In 1631 the Society equipped an expedition by Captain Thomas James in search of the North-West Passage.

6

EVENTS FROM THE SIXTEENTH TO NINETEENTH CENTURIES

During her short reign on the throne from 1553 until her death five years later, Mary I, who was Queen of England and Ireland, made vigorous attempts to return the Protestant Church of England back to Catholicism. The English Reformation had begun during the reign of her father, Henry VIII.

The Queen ordered that any of her subjects who refused to profess the Catholic faith should be burnt at the stake. All over the country nearly 300 people met their death this way.

In Bristol a church now stands on the site of a stake that was prominently sited at the top of St Michael's Hill, which leads up from the city centre to Cotham. Here five Marian Martyrs, as they became known, were burnt between 1555 and 1557.

Two memorial tablets at Cotham parish church – one on an inside wall and the other outside – tell of the death of five men for 'their avowal of the Christian faith'. Two of them were weavers; another was a shoemaker, a fourth man was a carpenter, while the occupation of the fifth man is not listed on the plaques.

The church itself was built in 1843 as Highbury Congregational Chapel to cater for the spiritual needs of the families who would be moving into new homes being built on the surrounding fields. The main benefactors of the church were William Day Wills and Henry Overton Wills of the Wills tobacco family.

THE CIVIL WAR

During the Civil War Bristol was regarded by both the Royalists and Parliamentarians as a potential stronghold. Prince Rupert of the Rhine, nephew of King Charles I and commander of the Royalist garrison in Bristol, took the city from Parliament in July 1643 at a cost of 500 lives. Prince Rupert's troops had broken through a weak point in the city's defences. The King visited the city the next day to thank his forces for capturing what then was England's second city.

Two years later Prince Rupert got word that a Parliamentary Army under General Sir Thomas Fairfax and Oliver Cromwell was making moves to recapture Bristol. Prince Rupert ordered that the villages around the city, including Clifton, should be burnt to the ground, which would prevent the advancing army from finding anywhere to shelter. Clifton's parish church of St Andrew survived but by 1654 it had fallen into disrepair and was largely restored. The church was destroyed in the Second World War and never rebuilt.

After a siege lasting one day short of three weeks, Prince Rupert capitulated to Fairfax and Cromwell, who retook the city for Parliament. Bristol did not see any further action in the Civil War.

The city has an unusual reminder of the war – the remains of a brick gatehouse that was part of the Royal

Fort, a pentagonal bastion in Clifton reconstructed by Prince Rupert after capturing Bristol in 1643.

RIDING INTO CHURCH HISTORY

Bristol has an important place in the history of Methodism for it was here that its founder John Wesley built the first Methodist chapel in the world, known as the 'New Room'. Within three months of arriving in the city in 1739 he had bought a plot of land near the Horsefair, on which his chapel, with its double-decker pulpit, still stands.

As well as being a place of worship, the 'New Room' had a schoolroom where teachers organised lessons for poor children who could not read or write. There was also a dispensary where the poor could get medicine. John Wesley also built a stable where visiting preachers could keep their horses.

A deed dated 29 June 1739 records the sale of the land to Wesley for £52 plus a chief rent of 1s a year. Within a month of work on the 'New Room' being completed the first service was held within its walls. In 1748 the New Room was extensively rebuilt and enlarged, and today it is known as the 'cradle of Methodism'.

Shortly after arriving in the city, John Wesley preached his first sermon to what he described in his journal as 'a little Society in Nicholas Street'. Shortly afterwards he delivered his first open-air sermon in a brickyard in St Philips when about 3,000 people gathered to hear him.

From then on Bristol was the starting point for Wesley's lengthy preaching tours and played a major part in the development of the Methodist Church. It was from here that Wesley set forth on horseback on tours that took him to Devon and Cornwall, through the Midlands to the north of England, to Wales and Ireland. Altogether Wesley travelled 250,000 miles and preached 40,000 sermons.

John Wesley kept a journal in which he recorded that on one visit he narrowly escaped injury. Wesley and his horse were knocked to the ground by the shaft of a cart, while passing out of a narrow gateway. He attributed his escape from injury to 'divine intervention'. In another journal entry he wrote, 'I often wonder at the people of Bristol. They are so honest and yet so dull, 'tis scarce possible to strike any fire into them.'

His ties with Bristol were further strengthened in 1749 when his brother Charles and his wife Sarah moved into a five-storey house near the 'New Room'. Charles lived in the house until 1771, writing many of his well-loved hymns there. He is credited with writing some 6,500 hymns, including the ever-popular 'Love Divine, All Loves Excelling' and the Christmas carol 'Hark the Herald Angels Sing'.

While living in Bristol, Charles' wife gave birth to a son, Samuel, who by the age of 5 years could read music. Three years later he had composed an oratorio called 'Ruth'.

John Wesley's 'New Room' today finds itself sandwiched between large department stores but is still a focal point for thousands of pilgrims who come from all over the world each year. Outside the chapel is a statue of Charles Wesley on horseback. From one small quaint church building in the centre of Bristol, the Methodist Church has rapidly grown both in the number of worshippers and in church buildings, of which there are now more than 6,000 in Britain.

TOLLS AND TURNPIKES

Roads in Britain were in such a ruinous state in the eighteenth century that travel had become a severe ordeal.

Indeed, a reader of *The Gentleman's Magazine* sent a letter to the editor complaining about the state of the Great West Road (the main road from Bristol to London now known as the A4). The writer described the road as 'the worst possible public road in all Europe'.

To help overcome the problem an Act of Parliament was passed in 1727, appointing the Members of Parliament for Bristol, Gloucestershire and Somerset along with Justices of the Peace and certain gentry to act as trustees for roads in their locality. The Turnpike Trusts, as they were called, were given authority to levy tolls for the upkeep and repair

One of the many toll-keepers' houses in Bristol

of the highway. The money was collected by toll-keepers, who kept watch from their specially built turnpike houses at intervals along the road.

The Bristol Turnpike Trust was one of the earliest in the country with tolls being first collected on 26 June 1727. This became one of the largest turnpike networks in England, being responsible for the western end of the Great Western Road along with a network of highways radiating into the market towns and coalfields of north Somerset and South Gloucestershire. Nearly twenty toll houses were built on the main roads leading in and out of Bristol.

A scale of charges carved on a board at a turnpike house just north of the city informed road users that the fee for every 'horse, mule, ass or any beast drawing a vehicle, except a stage coach' was 4*d*. A coach carrying up to nine passengers was charged 6*d* for each horse. If there were more than nine passengers, the charge was increased to 8*d* a horse. A 'drove of oxen were charged 10d a score, pigs, sheep and lambs 5d'. A wagon and six horses was charged 1*s*.

As these tolls were charged every 6 or 8 miles along the road, travel was both slow and expensive. The tolls were most unpopular with road users, especially the farmers and colliers who were travelling from the countryside into Bristol to sell their goods. Their immediate reaction was to pull down the toll gates as they approached them. On one occasion a mob from Somerset marched towards Bristol and when they reached the toll gates at Bedminster Down (now part of the city) they attacked them with hatchets and axes.

When tolls were introduced on Bristol Bridge, citizens again took the law into their own hands, but this time (1793) they decided to cause a riot. A mob of protesters who gathered on the bridge not only broke down its toll-gates but also set fire to the toll houses. The rioting went on for several days, with the magistrates reading the Riot Act to the mob, not just once but three times. However, their efforts at trying to disperse the crowd had no effect. The militia were called in and fired into the mob. Eleven people were killed and a further forty-five suffered various injuries. The authorities eventually decided to drop the tolls. Towards the end of the century, tolls across England were abolished and the cost of maintaining the major highways fell on to the shoulders of the newly created county councils. By this time the Bristol Turnpike Trust was looking after nearly 200 miles of public highway.

THE REFORM BILL RIOT

Feelings about the Reform Bill being debated in Parliament in 1831 were running high in Bristol, especially after the House of Lords defeated it even though the House of Commons had voted in favour. Had the Bill successfully passed through both Houses, the electoral system would have been changed, giving more people the right to vote.

There was strong feeling against Bristol's senior judge, the Recorder Sir Charles Wetherell, who had opposed the Bill in the House of Lords.

For three days and three nights after the Bill's defeat in October the centre of Bristol was the scene of some of the worst rioting witnessed in England in the nineteenth century. Public and private buildings were razed to the ground, others looted, and prisoners released from jail by the rioters.

When Recorder Wetherell arrived in Bristol to open a new session of the assize courts on 29 October, trouble soon broke out. The *Bristol Gazette* reported that as the judge approached the city along the Bath Road 'at a rapid rate in a chariot drawn by four greys, and stopping at Totterdown for the purpose of being handed into the Sheriff's carriage he was instantly assaulted by the most dreadful yells groans and hisses'.

After opening the assizes, the Recorder made his way to the Mayor's Mansion House in Queen Square where he would be entertained. The *Bristol Gazette* reported that rioters had already gathered there and were attacking the Mansion House and smashing its windows. Describing the scene the newspaper said that the rioters, having battered down the Mansion House door, went on to break into the Mayor's wine cellar 'and it is supposed that at least one-third of a stock of 300 dozen bottles of choice wines was carried off and wasted and drunk by the mob'.

It was deemed expedient for the Recorder to leave the Mansion House by escaping over the rooftops of adjoining houses. He left Bristol under the cover of darkness. Meanwhile, the Mayor and his officials were besieged.

The west side of Queen Square destroyed in the Reform Bill riot

As the rioting continued, two sides of Queen Square were soon in flames. Some of the rioters went on to destroy the Bishop of Bristol's palace at the back of the cathedral. Several hundred others armed with hatchets, crow bars and sledge-hammers broke away from the main mob and advanced to the Bristol Gaol in nearby Cumberland Road, which had been built ten years earlier. The mob pulled down the prison gates, giving a small boy the opportunity to get behind them and withdraw the bolts. The inevitable happened, with nearly 200 inmates escaping. Both prisoners and rioters then set light to the governor's house, the chapel and the prison's treadmill as well as its rooftop gallows. A large number of special constables were called in along with the militia to quell the crowd but without success.

The *Bristol Gazette* reported that hundreds of thousands of pounds worth of damage had been caused by the rioters. More than 100 of the mob were taken to court accused of rioting. Some reports at the time say that eighty-one of them

The north side of Queen Square after the Reform Bill riot

were convicted. Five of those were sentenced to death and another seven were transported to Australia. Others were sent to prison with or without hard labour. One defendant was reprieved on the grounds of insanity. Lieutenant-Colonel Brereton, who had sent the 14th Dragoons away from the rioting on the Saturday night, was also in court. He was charged with failing to keep the rioters down. However, at the end of the fourth day of the trial when evidence against Brereton was mounting he went home and committed suicide by shooting himself.

It is unclear how many people were killed, wounded or perished during the rioting.

A year after the riots, both the House of Commons and the House of Lords agreed to the Reform Bill. It meant that so-called 'Rotten Boroughs' were removed and more people could vote. At the time the riot was described as the worst outbreak of urban rioting since the Gordon Riots in London some fifty years earlier.

Several days before the disturbances in Queen Square, protesters were out in force when the Bishop of Bath and Wells consecrated the newly built St Paul's church on Coronation Road, Southville. Protesters who didn't like the bishop's opposition to the Reform Bill threw stones and mud at his carriage as he arrived at the church. Despite the noise of the protesters, the service of consecration of the church went ahead. Afterwards, some of those at the service escorted the bishop back to his carriage to make sure he got away safely.

7

SPRINGS AND SPAS

People flocked to spas during the eighteenth and nineteenth centuries, not only to 'take the waters' but also to be seen at these fashionable establishments. A social culture had built up around the spas with their ornate pump rooms and a master of ceremonies who hosted balls, banquets, concerts, card games and public breakfasts. The siting of the Hotwell Spa meant that river excursions and moonlight rowing parties on the River Avon were also available.

Any eagle-eyed celebrity spotter around the spa would have seen a 'Who's Who' of royalty, aristocrats and the literati all 'taking the waters'. Visitors were attracted by claims that the spring water of the Hot Well could cure a catalogue of illnesses including gout, diabetes and tuberculosis. Even doctors were recommending that the terminally ill use the spa. One medical man said that 'taking the waters' at the Hot Well would be good for those with 'hot livers, feeble brains and pimply faces'. Water from the spring became so popular that it was bottled and sold in cities like London and Oxford as well as overseas.

Chemical analysis of the water showed the presence of large amounts of mineral elements including carbonic acid, nitrogen, chloride of magnesium, nitrate of magnesia, chloride of sodium, sulphates of soda, magnesium and lime, carbonates of lime, magnesia and iron.

Water from the spring on the bank of the River Avon at the foot of St Vincent's Rocks, close to the Clifton Suspension Bridge, was gushing out at 60 gallons a minute with a temperature of 76°F (24°C).

As the number of visitors increased, the spring was enclosed in the specially built Hotwell House, which stood on a rock ledge jutting out into the River Avon. Water was raised by pumps into the pump room above. The lessee of Hotwell House paid a yearly rental to the Society of Merchant Venturers, the landlords of the Manor of Clifton.

The Hot Well spring was first mentioned in 1480 by the topographer William Worcester in his *Inventory*, although he did not comment on any health-giving property the water may have had. Among the many notable visitors were the writer Joseph Addison, and poets William Cowper and Alexander Pope. The poet William Whitehead was so impressed by what he had seen that he wrote 'A Hymn to the Nymph of the Bristol Spring'. Tobias Smollett set the opening of his novel *Humphry Clinker* at the spa, while the traveller and writer Celia Fiennes described the water as 'warm as new milk and much of that sweetness'.

Catherine of Braganza, the Queen Consort of Charles II, was the first royal to sample what she described as the 'rare excellency of these waters'. The Duke of York and the Duchess of Marlborough were also visitors.

To meet the spiritual needs of those who visited the spa, an Episcopal chapel was built in nearby Dowry Square, while some of their secular requirements were met by a row of shops known as The Colonnade that was built at the foot of the Avon Gorge. One shop was occupied by Ann Yearsley, a local milkmaid turned poet, who invested earnings from her verses into running a library. The shops have long gone but The Colonnade itself remains and is the only reminder we now have of the Hotwell Spa.

The existence of the spa sparked a house-building boom on the hillside that climbs up to Clifton village. Landlords let many of the new houses as lodgings for those going to the spa.

An unusual event happened in 1755 when the spa water turned deep red and could not be consumed. Its discoloration was put down to a side effect of an earthquake that shook Lisbon.

The popularity of the spa declined as quickly as it rose, with rising prices partly to blame. It had also acquired something of a sinister reputation of being the last resort of the incurable. So many people died here that in 1787 a new graveyard had to be dug on Lower Clifton Hill. It became known as the 'Strangers Burial Ground', simply because no one knew who the deceased were or from where they came.

Hotwell House was demolished in 1822 so that Bridge Valley Road linking Hotwells with Clifton could be built.

LADY HOPE'S WILL

Typical of the visitors to Hotwell Spa were Lady Henrietta Hope and her friend Lady Wilhema Glenorchy. The couple, from Edinburgh, were travelling around the country taking the waters at various spas. The couple arrived at the Hot Well in 1785.

Another of Lady Hope's interests was promoting the cause of religion. To this end she left her mark on the Hot Well district with her plans to build a chapel near the spa. However, she died before construction work could start. In her will she had left £2,500 for the project to go ahead, so Lady Glenorchy took on the task of building the chapel.

Unfortunately, she too did not live long enough to see it built. That task then fell to her executors.

Hope Chapel, built for Calvinistic evangelical worship, opened with room for 900 worshippers. It still stands on Hope Chapel Hill and is now the home of Hope Community church.

Rival Spas

For those who wanted to give the hurly-burly of the Hotwell Spa a miss, there was a quieter and much smaller spa further along the Avon Gorge, past the Clifton Suspension Bridge. It became known as the New Hotwell and it was here that John Wesley, founder of the Methodist Church, is said to have visited to improve his health. One of the spa's lessees wrote in a publicity leaflet that Wesley's 'countenance looked as if a greedy consumption had determined to put an end to his days'. However, within a couple of weeks of arriving at the spa, Wesley was said to have been preaching every day. By the end of the century, the pump house was in ruins.

Meanwhile, Thomas Morgan, an attorney living on Sion Hill, Clifton, drilled a borehole 250ft down through the limestone rock and tapped a spring with warm water in 1793. He used a steam engine to pump up the water to a room he had built for visitors along with a reading room, but his venture proved to be unprofitable.

By 1811 Thomas Morgan was supplying the water from his Sion Spring to some 300 homes nearby through supply pipes that had been specially installed. Iron traps, which can still be seen in the pavements of Caledonia Place, gave access to cisterns where residents stored their water. Eventually, Sion Spring was sold for £13,500 to the newly formed Bristol Waterworks company.

Morgan's Pump Room was replaced by the forty-four-room St Vincent's Rocks Hotel. That ceased trading in 2002 when the building was converted into the present private houses and apartments.

TRAVELLING THROUGH THE ROCKS

Buried inside the rocks of the Avon Gorge is the only underground cliff railway in the world. It was the answer to the prayers of those who wanted a transport link between Hotwells, at the foot of the gorge, and Clifton, rising more than 200ft above ground level. The railway was built without destroying the natural beauty of the rugged rock face.

It was the idea of George Newnes, a Member of Parliament, businessman and publisher of magazines such as *The Strand*. He was the main financial backer of the funicular railway linking the towns of Lynton and Lynmouth on the rugged cliff face of the north Devon coast.

The Society of Merchant Venturers, who owned the ground, approved of Newnes' idea, which included building a grand pump room and spa for using the mineral waters of the springs in the area. His tunnel through the carboniferous limestone rocks formed a direct and straight connection between Hotwells and Clifton. It rose a distance of 240ft, climbing at a vertical rise of 1ft for every 2.2ft.

It took the builders two years to cut and blast through the limestone, install the track and build stations at the top and the bottom of the cliff. The total cost of £30,000 was met solely by Newnes. The water-powered railway opened on 11 March 1893. On the first day 6,200 passengers passed through the turnstiles for the return trip.

For nearly four decades the light blue and white passenger carriages decorated with gold lettering ran up and down the tunnel. However, the popularity of the railway then started to decline and in 1934 the Rocks Railway closed. The carriages were lowered to the bottom station and later removed. Meanwhile, a group of preservationists have been restoring what they can and holding open days for visitors keen to view what remains of the railway.

A Spa for Clifton

To build a spa with a pump room for Clifton, George Newnes converted three houses at the end of Princes Buildings. Apart from guests taking the spa water, Newnes wanted his patrons to enjoy lunchtime concerts, too. His project came to fruition in 1894 with water being pumped up some 240ft though the rocks of the Avon Gorge. Russian, Turkish, douche, hydro, steam, massage and electrical baths were provided for guests in their private suites.

Newnes' Grand Clifton Spa and Hydropathic Institution received a civic seal of approval when it was officially opened with a formal dinner attended by the Lady Mayoress of Bristol and 700 specially invited guests. Many of them had been selected as they circulated in influential and wealthy social circles from which Newnes hoped to draw some of his patrons. After dinner the guests were entertained with music from the 1st Band of the Life Guards and singing from Madame Strathearn.

One newspaper reported that the spa was 'one of the best in the kingdom'. Its medical director had carried out research at spas on the Continent to bring the latest ideas back to Bristol. A guide book published in 1902 noted that the pump room had 'twenty massive pillars of Cipollino marble'. It seems that money was no object in providing guests with the best facilities.

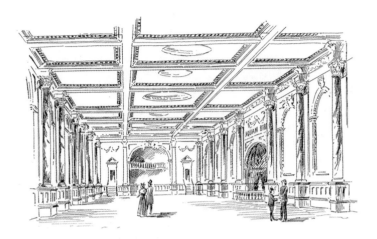

Interior of the Pump Room in Clifton

At one time up to 300 people were drinking the water each day. However, by the early 1920s the popularity of the spa was waning and Newnes' spa ceased operating. The pump room became a cinema, although that too had a relatively short life. What was the pump room is still there but the days of people taking the waters are long gone.

8

A TRIANGULAR TRADE

The eighteenth century in Bristol will always be remembered as the era of the infamous triangular shipping trade, which was more commonly known as the slave trade. Trinkets and cotton items were among the goods that went out from Bristol to Africa in exchange for slaves, who were then taken to the plantations of America and the West Indies while sugar, rum and tobacco were brought back home in the same ships.

To Bristol's everlasting shame, it became heavily committed to the trade. Its involvement began when a ship, perhaps appropriately named *The Beginning*, sailed to the west coast of Africa in 1698. Between then and 1807 a known 2,108 slaver ships left Bristol. The exact number of local ships involved in the trade will probably never be known. However, it has been estimated that nearly 500,000 slaves were carried on these vessels in the most appalling of conditions. The bodies of slaves who died on the journey were unceremoniously thrown overboard into the sea.

Bristol became one of the main ports in the United Kingdom involved in the slave trade. The profits from the trade made Bristol, an already wealthy city, even more prosperous.

Contrary to public opinion, very few slaves were brought back to Bristol. However, Pero Jones, who was born enslaved on the Caribbean island of Nevis and of African descent, was brought to the city. When he was 12 years old Pero was bought by Bristol merchant John Pinney to work on his Mountravers plantation on Nevis. Pinney later brought Pero Jones to his eighteenth-century home in Great George Street, where he was a domestic servant for the next thirty-two years. As far as we know, Pero was never given his freedom; he lived and died a slave.

What became Pero's home is known today as the Georgian House; a museum with its eleven rooms spread over four floors revealing what life was like above and below stairs. Visitors can see the kitchen in the basement where servants prepared meals for Pinney and his family in the elegant formal rooms upstairs.

A footbridge that was built in 1999 spanning St Augustine's Reach in the Floating Harbour is named after Pero as a tribute to the many unknown African men, women and children who were enslaved by merchants of Bristol.

SLAVERY AND PHILANTHROPY

Until recently it was almost impossible to be unaware of the name and fame of the man who was probably Bristol's most prominent slave trader. Stroll around the city and you would find a number of schools, a dozen or so streets, a pub, a concert hall and an office block named after Edward Colston. Stained glass windows commemorating him were installed in several churches. A statue of a rather pensive-looking Colston leaning on a stick stood on a plinth in busy Colston Avenue, in the centre of the city, with thousands of commuters and visitors passing by each day, many of them photographing the bronze memorial.

Colston (1636–1721) was born into a wealthy Bristol merchant family. By 1672 he had his own business in London which traded in slaves, cloth, wine and sugar. In 1680 Colston became an official of the Royal African Company, which at the time held the monopoly in Britain for slave trading. Although he lived in the capital for many years Colston remained closely associated with his native city.

Statue of Edward Colston in Colston Avenue

He gave almost £80,000 to charity in Bristol – a vast amount in those days – and established almshouses and schools, which were named after him. He also restored a number of churches, not only in Bristol but in other parts of the country as well. In the year that he died Colston gave the ancient church of All Saints in Corn Street £250 towards the cost of adding a classic cupola to the tower. Colston was buried in All Saints where a rather grand monument includes a long list of his bequests – but there is no mention of his slaving activities. Colston's philanthropy was possibly why he was revered so much in his home-city.

In recent years Colston's statue became the subject of much controversy. One petition signed by 1,100 people called for it to be removed. The bronze statue was erected in 1895 with a plaque on the plinth stating: 'Erected by the citizens of Bristol as a memorial to one of the most virtuous and wise sons of their city'. Bristol City Council faced many calls for a second plaque to be added to the plinth mentioning Colston's slave-trading activities. However, it never happened.

A symbolic moment and a signal for change in the city came on the afternoon of Sunday 7 June 2020, when protestors gathered around Colston's statue with some of them bringing it to the ground using ropes and chains. The statue was then rolled through the city centre and dramatically dumped into the Floating Harbour. This historic event made newspaper, radio and television headlines around the world. The toppling of the statue happened as an estimated 10,000 people gathered in the centre of Bristol for a Black Lives Matter protest.

Four days later, shortly after dawn, the statue was salvaged from the harbour by the city council, which said that it would later be displayed in one of its museums.

All Saints church, Corn Street

The force of energy in Bristol that followed the actions of the protestors made the headlines in its own right. The owners of a multi-storey office block known as Colston Tower which stood beside the statue had the name quickly removed from the building. Officials of the neighbouring Colston Hall, the city's largest music venue, also removed its brand name – in another early morning operation. In 2017 trustees of the hall announced that it would have a new name when an on-going £45 million rebuild was completed. After the statue was toppled it was announced that the hall would in future be known as the Bristol Beacon. The Bishop of Bristol, the Rt Rev. Vivienne Faull, revealed work had started on removing a number of prominent references to Edward Colston in both Bristol Cathedral and St Mary Redcliffe church. Colston commemoration windows had long been installed in both places of worship. Schools that were named after Colston set about changing their identities after consultations which included governors, pupils, parents and staff. The Society of Merchant Venturers, of which Edward Colston was a member, issued a statement saying that the removal of the statue from its plinth 'was right for Bristol'.

Announcing the launch of a Local History Commission, the Mayor of Bristol, Marvin Rees, said: 'It does suggest that it is time for the city to take a long hard look at its history and have a period of reckoning and reflection.'

He said he and his fellow commissioners were 'doing this for free' and expected it would take a couple of years. A council spokesperson said the commission would include the building and removal of the Colston statue as a departure point and would also consider the growth of education, the struggles of workers for pay and working conditions, and the Chartists and suffragettes campaigning for emancipation.

The spokesman added: 'The key roles of wars, protests, the harbour and the docks, manufacturing and industry, research and innovation, transport, slum clearances, housing, modern gentrification, migration and faith in the development of the city will also be within the commission's scope.'

THE FIGHT AGAINST SLAVERY

Many people across Bristol were opposed to slavery and a petition started in the city in the seventeenth century attracted nearly 1,000 signatures. Many notable citizens made their views in favour of abolition widely known. One of them was the Bristol-born educator and social reformer Hannah More, who wrote about slavery in some of her poems. She also encouraged women to join the anti-slavery campaign. Bristol-born Poet Laureate Robert Southey also used his pen to attack slavery.

Abolitionist Thomas Clarkson, the son of a vicar and a Cambridge-educated clergyman himself, arrived in the city in 1787 to collect information about the notorious slave trade. He was welcomed by the landlord of the Seven Stars public house in Redcliffe who introduced him to disgruntled sailors who had worked on slave ships. He also showed him some of the dockside pubs that helped to recruit for the trade. As so much of Bristol's money was tied up with slavery, Clarkson risked life and limb just being in the city. Many of his meetings had to take place under the cover of darkness.

During his inquiries, Clarkson collected equipment used on the slave ships such as iron handcuffs, leg shackles and branding irons. He passed all these items and the information he had gathered to his friend William Wilberforce, the Member of Parliament for Hull, who was one of the Parliamentary leaders against the slave trade. A Parliamentary bill for its abolition eventually received

Royal Assent in 1807 and slavery itself was banned throughout the British Empire a quarter of a century later.

Clarkson published a book, *History of the Abolition of the African Slave Trade*, which included much of his research in Bristol. He worked relentlessly as an anti-slavery campaigner and this is marked by a multi-coloured, bas-relief moulded plaque on the exterior wall of the Seven Stars. It carries the heading 'Cry Freedom, Cry Seven Stars' and has a portrait of Clarkson surrounded by scenes from his campaign.

9

THE VICTORIAN YEARS

MAN OF IRON

By the start of the Victorian era, Bristol was still growing but had lost its place as second city in the country after London. It had not experienced growth on the large scale that happened in the Midlands and the North of England during the years of the Industrial Revolution.

However, as far as the people of Bristol were concerned, the nineteenth century could well have belonged to one man, the great Victorian engineer Isambard Kingdom Brunel. On 19 July 1837, a month after Queen Victoria ascended the throne when she was just 18 years old, Brunel's SS *Great Western*, the world's first ocean-going liner, was launched in Bristol's docks. Brunel designed the ship for the North Atlantic mail and passenger service. The following April it sailed to New York. The SS *Great Western* made a total of sixty-seven Atlantic journeys and was awarded the Atlantic Blue Riband, an unofficial accolade given to the passenger liner with the record highest speed for crossing the Atlantic Ocean in regular service – in this case fourteen days. The ship was later sold to the Royal Mail Company, which owned it for many years before it was broken up.

Six years after the launch of the SS *Great Western*, Brunel's SS *Great Britain* was floated out of the berth in which it was built into the water of the Bristol docks. Tickets were sold for this event and large crowds gathered around the shipyard where the ship had been constructed. This was the first iron-built vessel propelled by screw propeller that had been built for ocean-going service. It was initially designed to carry around 250 passengers with a crew of 130 men but was later adapted to accommodate more than 700 travellers. With a length of 320ft and a width of 50ft this was the biggest ship in the world at the time.

Queen Victoria's husband, Prince Albert, launched the SS *Great Britain*. According to the *Bristol Mirror*, two bottles of champagne were needed for the ceremonial launch. The first bottle that Prince Albert swung at the ship's hull somehow missed its target. However, a second bottle was conveniently at hand and given to the Prince. This time the bottle hit the right spot.

The SS *Great Britain* was in service for nearly forty-five years, clocking up more than a million miles. During her chequered career the ship was used as a troop ship in the Crimean War, a liner carrying emigrants to Australia and even to transport coal to San Francisco. The SS *Great Britain* ended its life on the seas rather ignominiously as a floating warehouse for storing wool and coal before it was scuttled at Sparrow Cove, off the Falkland Islands. It stayed there for thirty-three years before being towed back to Bristol for restoration and a new career as a tourist attraction.

THE FIRST TRAIN CALLING AT TEMPLE MEADS

Monday, 31 August 1840 was a momentous day for Bristol. This was when Isambard Kingdom Brunel brought his Great Western Railway to Bristol. The original Great Western Railway Terminus at Temple Meads, also designed by Brunel, opened at the same time, with the first passenger train leaving the station for Bath at 8 a.m. Other destinations would soon be available as the number of railway companies using Temple Meads station increased.

Many thousands of people thronged around Temple Meads station, which was bedecked in banners and flags, so that they could get sight of the Fireball locomotive, which was pulling six carriages, three of them for first-class passengers and two for second-class travellers The Fireball was designed by the Great Western Railway's Chief Engineer, Daniel Gooch, and belonged to the Firefly Class of locomotive that could reach speeds of more than 60mph.

None of the spectators that morning could get a ticket for the first train to Bath as all the 300 seats had been allocated by the Great Western Railway to special guests. They included directors of the firm, their families and friends as well as Bristol's civic dignitaries. It was not until later in the day that those early morning spectators could get a trip on one of the ten services that were running the 13 miles to Bath on the first day. Such was the interest in this historic event that people crowded on to bridges along the route to get a good view of the train.

The opening of the station came almost a year before the first through train from London to Bristol arrived. Isambard Kingdom Brunel was building the Great Western Railway in separate stages, with the first stretch of the line running from Paddington to Maidenhead.

A significant feature of his original terminus is the train shed that, for the first time for a railway station, was roofed with a single span constructed of timber. Today the roof covers a car park for railway travellers.

Strangely, Temple Meads station does not have a statue of Brunel on any of its platforms. There is nothing to tell visitors that they have arrived in 'Brunel land' – the city where the master engineer built not only a railway, but also bridges and ships, and helped to remodel the docks. There is a statue of him, though, outside the offices of the firm of solicitors who did much of Brunel's legal work connected with the railway. It stands on the newly developed business quarter of Temple Quay. An identical life-size statue of Brunel stands on Platform 1 at Paddington, London, the eastern end of the Great Western Railway. The companion statues, sculpted by John Doubleday, were both unveiled on the same day in May 1982.

TIME FOR A CHANGE

Before the growth of the railways most people expected to spend their lives close to home. Travel by stagecoach was slow and the uneven surface of the roads gave passengers anything but a smooth ride. The Great Western Railway Company soon began to tempt local people to travel by train; they could reach the capital in hours rather than the days needed if they went by stagecoach.

The expansion of the railway meant changes to the time-keeping method used across the country. In the early Victorian days there was no such thing as Standard Time; every city and town had its own local time reckoned by the sun and signalled by church bells.

Bristol lies 2 degrees and 36 minutes west of the Greenwich Meridian, meaning that the sun reaches its noon peak eleven minutes later than at Greenwich. If Bristolians wanted to catch a train at midday they had to remember that it would leave the platform at Temple Meads at 11.49 a.m. Bristol Time. To make things easier, Bristol Corporation arranged for the main public clock on the façade of the Exchange in Corn Street to show both local and Greenwich Mean Time by adding an extra second hand to the clock face to show local time. Bristol finally adopted Greenwich Mean Time in 1852. However, the Exchange clock still shows local time as well as GMT.

LIFE ON THE DOWNS

Three years before Brunel's Clifton Suspension Bridge was opened, its very near neighbour, the Clifton and Durdham Downs, was the subject of an Act of Parliament that ensured the grassland 'shall forever be kept open and unenclosed as a place of public resort'.

Several hundred years ago the Downs, as they are affectionately known by the people of Bristol, were a dangerous and desolate place. This open parkland of more than 400 acres was the haunt of highwaymen and footpads. The *Bristol Journal* reported in 1819 that 'roads leading to Clifton are so infested at night with desperadoes that few gentlemen think it safe to walk about alone or unarmed'.

One of the most notorious footpads was Jenkin Protheroe, who lurked about the Downs ingratiating himself with kind-hearted passing travellers. Having gained their confidence he would then attack and rob them. On one occasion his victim died and Protheroe was gibbeted for murder. The gibbet stood on the highest spot of the Downs at the top of the present Pembroke Road, then known as Gallows Acre Lane. The bodies of murderers were often left to rot swinging from the gibbet. Legend has it that the ghost of Protheroe, who was hanged in 1783, still haunts the spot. Protheroe had the rather dubious distinction of being the last person to be hanged on the gibbet at Gallows Acre Lane.

At one time the Downs had two owners. The Society of Merchant Venturers were the owners of Clifton Down, which runs up to the edge of the Avon Gorge clifftop, while the Lords of the Manor of Henbury owned Durdham Downs, to the north. Mini tombstones across the parkland mark the old dividing line. The Merchants were keen that the Downs should be made available for the pleasure and recreation of the people of Bristol in perpetuity and gave their share to Bristol Corporation. The Lords of the Manor of Henbury followed suit in giving up their part of the Downs but in return for the sum of £15,000.

The Downs are now administered by a committee of six Merchant Venturers and six city councillors, who meet regularly to discuss day-to-day management of the site. One tradition that overrides any rules made about use of the land is the right to graze sheep here, first granted in an Anglo-Saxon charter. This right still exists for almost twenty commoners, including individuals and several schools on the edge of the Downs, as well as the University of Bristol. In some cases the right came to the present owners by way of property acquisition, and in others it was a right that was inherited. An Act of Parliament states that as long as the Downs remains a common – and sheep grazing is one legal proof of that – the land cannot be built upon. From time to time commoners still put sheep on Durdham Downs to maintain their right and keep up what is now regarded as an unusual tradition. There were once up to 2,000 sheep there, but grazing had generally died out by 1924 following an outbreak of sheep scab. The manager of an hotel on the edge of the Downs also complained that the bleating of sheep was an annoyance to his guests.

Through the centuries calamine, lead and stone have been quarried on the Downs. There was a big demand for stone to build the large villas on the fringe of the grassland for wealthy merchants, who were moving away from the industrial grime, noise and smoke of the town centre for cleaner air and a healthier life.

Many sporting activities have taken place on the Downs. Gloucestershire County Cricket Club played a match against Surrey on Durdham Down before moving to a permanent site at the County Ground in Horfield. Gloucestershire won the match by 51 runs.

By all accounts the most popular sport was the annual horse racing staged on an improvised course from around 1738 until 1838. The Durdham Down Races attracted large crowds of spectators. For winning horses and their jockeys there were trophies and cash prizes; sometimes as much as 100 sovereigns. A contemporary newspaper report said that, 'The carriages were very numerous and filled with beautiful and elegant females which presented one of the most delightful scenes the imagination could portray.' Alexander Pope, satirist and poet, talked about the 'fine turf' and 'delicious walking and riding there'.

A part of the grassland was once taken over for carpet beating long before the invention of vacuum cleaners. Domestic servants working in the nearby villas took carpets on to the Downs and beat them against posts that were specially erected for the purpose. A by-law was eventually introduced in 1892 banning this activity after complaints from people enjoying a walk in the fresh air that it was a nuisance. The problem got worse when commercial carpet-beating companies joined the local residents. Other by-laws ban swearing, fighting and the hanging up of washing for drying.

Clifton and Durdham Downs, also known as Bristol's 'green lung', are now a well-loved venue for everyone from sportspeople to dog walkers and from kite-flyers to bird watchers – especially those trying to spot peregrine falcons, which are breeding once again in the Avon Gorge after a long absence.

'MY FIRST CHILD, MY DARLING'

The opening of Clifton Suspension Bridge attracted one of the biggest crowds the city had ever seen in the Victorian era. Countless thousands of people lined the streets and hillsides around the bridge to witness its official opening on 8 December 1864. They could have been forgiven for thinking that this day might never come.

Although construction work on the bridge started in 1831, it stopped several times because of financial problems. A

Clifton Suspension Bridge under construction

Bristol wine merchant, William Vick, had bequeathed £1,000 in his will for a stone bridge to be built across the Avon Gorge. He instructed that his bequest should be invested together with its accumulated interest until it reached £10,000. William Vick thought this would cover the cost of building a bridge. In the event the cost was £100,000.

Brunel was the first person to make a crossing of the gorge under the bridge. This was in a basket slung from an iron bar attached to the unfinished bridge to carry workmen from one side of the Avon Gorge to the other. Soon this unusual form of transport attracted many curious passengers, who were charged 5s for the first trip across the gorge and 2s 6d if they made the return journey. On one occasion a honeymoon couple were stranded in the middle of the Avon Gorge for several hours when one of the basket's hauling ropes snapped and had to be repaired.

In his journal, Brunel described the bridge as 'my first child, my darling'. Unfortunately, he died five years before work on it was finished. The bridge was completed by his fellow workmen as a monument in memory of him.

Besides organised firework displays marking the opening of the bridge, spectators let off their own sparklers and squibs. Apparently this bit of entertainment brought its own risks, for one man reported 'ruthless burning of the whiskers on one side only'.

The *Illustrated London News* reported that the opening ceremony 'was attended with much festivity and pomp'. Its reporter noted that:

There was a procession through the city of Bristol, composed of all the trades and benefit societies, bearing the banners and models illustrative of various callings. This procession, which came early, was immense in numbers, and took nearly three hours to wind through Bristol to the

Clifton Suspension Bridge in progress

edge of the Clifton ravine, whence they wound down by the 'zigzag' (narrow path linking Clifton with Hotwells below).

There was another and more dignified procession, which came precisely at twelve o'clock to perform the actual ceremony. This procession did not arrive upon the ground till all the spectators and visitors were assembled – that is to say, till the approaches to the bridge were filled, till the heights of Leigh Woods were crowded, and the ledge of steep grey cliffs lined with dense masses of people.

Captain Huish, chairman of the bridge company, was loudly cheered as he read a brief address setting out

The completed Clifton Suspension Bridge spanning the Avon
Gorge. The New Inn on the left has long gone.

the history of the undertaking. Prayers were said by the
Bishop of Gloucester, followed by speeches from local dignitaries and then the bridge was officially declared open.
Without wasting any time, 21-year-old Mary Griffiths
from Hanham in South Gloucestershire immediately ran
out of the crowd and across the 702ft span from pier to
pier. She went down in the history books as the first person
to cross Clifton Suspension Bridge.

It is not generally known that the Clifton end of the
bridge is 3ft higher than the other side. Brunel designed the
bridge that way to create a level appearance because of the
topography of the area.

Brunel could not have dreamt that his bridge would be
used as a focal point for all kinds of stunts. Several jet pilots
have flown their aircraft underneath it. However, in 1957
such an attempt ended in tragedy when the plane crashed
into the woods on the Somerset side of the Avon Gorge,

with the pilot losing his life. A bridge by-law that says that no one can use the bridge for 'parachuting, rope swinging, or bungee jumping' didn't deter four members of Oxford University's Dangerous Sports Society on April Fool's Day 1979. The four daredevils jumped off the bridge in a bungee jump stunt, to drink a champagne toast dangling halfway down the Avon Gorge hanging on to elasticated ropes.

One of the strangest stunts connected with the bridge was reported by the *Bristol Magpie Magazine* of February 1896. It said that quite a sensation was caused 'when it became known that Zanetto (a Japanese juggler) would catch on a small fork placed in his mouth, a turnip thrown from the bridge'. The magazine reported that, 'Some 5,000 persons assembled to see the wonderful feat, and after two or three failures, on account of the wind and the great height, the trick was successfully accomplished, amidst the enthusiastic applause of the assembled multitude.'

PACKING THE PEWS

During the Victorian era the people of Bristol were very religious and God fearing, as they were in other towns and cities. As the city's population grew, more churches were being built to cater for the spiritual needs of the people. A *Bristol Directory* brought out by J. Wright, printers, publishers and stationers, in 1875 listed more than 150 churches and chapels ranging from Bristol Cathedral to the Seamens' Floating Chapel, moored in the city docks, and from the Moravian Church to the Unitarian Church.

Typical of the newly built churches was All Saints on Pembroke Road, Clifton. It was erected on part of a field the Church of England authorities purchased from the Society of Merchant Venturers, landlords of the Manor of Clifton.

In its early days All Saints, which was consecrated in 1868, held seven services on a Sunday starting at 6 a.m. Services were also listed for every weekday. To seat the church-goers, rush-bottomed chairs were provided, with men sitting on one side of the church and women on the other.

One of Bristol's first suburbs to be laid out in the early eighteenth century was the St Paul's district, close to the city centre. The focal point of the elegant Portland Square was St Paul's church, known as the 'wedding cake church' because of its tiered tower. In its early years the church catered for the wealthy merchants who had moved into the suburb. It was at this church that the first performance took place in Bristol in 1803 of Handel's *Messiah*. The church became redundant in 1968 and now has a totally different use as a school for circus performers.

Religion played such a focal point in Victorian life that the *Western Daily Press* decided to conduct a census of church-going on Sunday, 30 October 1881. This turned out to be a most comprehensive survey for it not only took in sixty-nine Anglican churches but also those of other denominations including Roman Catholic, Welsh Calvinistic, Methodist and Primitive Methodist.

The census revealed that All Saints in Clifton, where the priest ministered to more than 500 worshippers at the early service and nearly 700 at the main morning service, was one of the busiest churches surveyed.

The *Western Daily Press* reported that the largest congregation though was at St Paul's church in Southville, where 2,316 church attendees were recorded. This included nearly 200 people who attended the early morning celebration of Holy Communion. It was noted that the 'absence of the vicar at St Paul's would no doubt have caused the congregation to be less than usual'. Almost 400 more people turned up at St Paul's mission rooms in Ashton Gate and at Albion Docks.

St Paul's church, known as the wedding cake church, in Portland Square

At Bristol Cathedral the clergy preached to 1,362 people at the morning service and at Evensong. Across the city at Old Market, almost 1,300 people packed the pews at St Philip and Jacob, trendily known today as Pip 'n' Jay. The census recorded that 'several people could not obtain admission to the evening service'.

The chapel at Her Majesty's Prison at Horfield was also included in the survey. Here 147 worshippers were in the chapel, although the census did not distinguish between prison warders and inmates. The Red, White and Blue

Temperance Army, with four meeting places across the city, counted a total of 523 people, while at the Seamen's Floating Chapel the clergy preached to a total of 267 people at two services. At the Royal Infirmary, seventy people made their way to the hospital's chapel, although again there was no distinction between staff and patients. The lowest attendance was said to be at the Swedenborgian church in Terrell Street, where just fifty-seven people were counted.

After the Church of England, the best-attended churches were those of the Congregationalists, followed by the Salvation Army. The *Western Daily Press* reported that on the last Sunday in October 1881 a total of 109,452 people had attended a service in Bristol.

The statistics were supplied by the clergy and analysed by the paper's editorial staff. It was estimated that a further 7,000 people living outside the city boundary had also gone to their local church or chapel.

Knighted on the Pavement

Most investitures held by the monarch normally take place in a royal residence such as Buckingham Palace. However, in November 1899 Queen Victoria came to Bristol and conferred a knighthood on Councillor Herbert Ashman, the city's first Lord Mayor, as opposed to Mayor. Mr Ashman was the head of a family firm of leather manufacturers and importers in the city. His name is carved in the pediment of a building in Broadmead that was for many years his firm's headquarters and later became the home of the *Bristol Evening Post* and the *Western Daily Press*. It housed printing presses and offices for both newspapers.

In her Queen's Birthday Honours List of June 1899, Queen Victoria, by virtue of Letters Patent, granted that Bristol's Mayor should in future be styled the Right Honourable the Lord Mayor. This was a big honour for the city as only seven other towns in England and Wales at the time had a Lord Mayor. It is a title that can only be granted by the monarch. The holder of this distinguished office has the honour due to an earl and takes precedence over everyone in the city, save for members of the royal family when they are visiting.

Queen Victoria had travelled by train to Temple Meads station and then by horse-drawn carriage for the mile or so journey to the administrative headquarters of Bristol Corporation (now city council) at the Council House, then in Corn Street, for the investiture ceremony.

However, the Queen did not enter the Council House, let alone leave her open-top carriage. The *Western Daily Press* reported that:

> The Royal carriage drew up in front of the stand and Sir Arthur Biggs was observed to have unsheathed his sword and passed it to HRH Duke of Connaught who occupied the seat opposite to Her Majesty in the carriage.
>
> The Queen then beckoned the Lord Mayor (Cllr Herbert Ashman) to kneel beside the carriage and having received the sword from the Duke of Connaught held it above the Lord Mayor's head and bade him to rise as Sir Herbert Ashman. This was the signal for another round of cheering.

It was probably the first – and maybe the last – time that someone knelt on the street pavement to be knighted, although it was covered by a red carpet. It may have been due to the Queen's frailty – she was then in her eightieth year – that she did not step down from her carriage.

After the investiture, the Queen travelled a couple of miles on to Clifton Down to open a new convalescent home named after her. It had been funded by the people of Bristol as a tribute to their monarch.

Queen Victoria sat in her carriage outside the home to perform the official opening ceremony. She pressed a button on a device that was attached to an electric wire, which in turn operated a magnet that had sufficient power to raise a clutch to open the building's main door.

On the edge of Clifton and Durdham Downs a stand had been specially erected to accommodate 27,500 school-children. At this spot the Queen's procession stopped for several minutes while the youngsters sang the National Anthem.

FAREWELL TO A GRAND OLD LADY

On 17 January 1901 the *Western Daily Press* reported on the state of Queen Victoria's health in just one paragraph. It didn't appear on the front page as any news of the royal family almost certainly does today. That prominent position in the newspaper was then reserved for fee-paying advertisements, mainly those of a classified nature. The news from the royal household about the Queen was virtually hidden on the middle page of the paper tucked away under the rather strange heading of 'Topics of the Day'. It read:

> It was officially announced last night that the strain upon the Queen during the past year has rather upset her Majesty's nervous system. Perfect quiet is ordered and Her Majesty abstains for the present from transacting business.

Five days later the paper told its readers that the Queen had died at the age of 81. She had ascended to the throne on

20 June 1837 when she was just 18 years old and spent sixty-three years, seven months and two days as monarch.

The Queen's death prompted a special meeting of the city council to be called, when a resolution of condolence was passed. On news of the Queen's passing, Bristol was plunged, like the rest of the country, into mourning. The *Western Daily Press* printed heavy black lines separating one column from another down its broadsheet pages. The paper did this every day until the Queen's funeral on 2 February.

A week after Queen Victoria's death, the *Clifton Chronicle* reported that, 'Signs of mourning are universal. Every social function has been abandoned and numerous events postponed.' The Lord Mayor and Sheriff, accompanied by other civic notables, paid their last respects to the Queen at a service of thanksgiving in Bristol Cathedral. So many citizens wanted to do the same that the cathedral authorities held several special services during the following week. One service alone had a choir of 500 voices. Services were also held at the Colston Hall.

Across the city parish churches, many of them draped in black, held their own acts of thanksgiving. Church bells rang muffled peals and wreaths were laid around the statue of Queen Victoria on College Green. Many streets across the city were later named in memory of the Queen. On the day of the Queen's funeral many citizens were dressed in the mourning colour of black.

Queen Victoria had only visited Bristol twice during her lifetime. The first occasion was as an 11-year-old princess. She stayed with her mother and members of the royal household at the Assembly Rooms hotel in The Mall, Clifton, now the home of the Clifton Club, while on a tour of the West Country. Reporting on the visit, the *Bristol Mirror* on 20 October 1830 said that:

A vast concourse of people assembled at Clifton to greet their arrival. The entrance to the hotel, where instructions had been sent to prepare for the reception of the royal party, was illuminated with lamps and surmounted by a transparency of the Royal Arms, encircled with laurel. The houses in the neighbourhood were also illuminated.

The paper's report continued:

The multitude took their hats off and received the royal party with the most enthusiastic cheers. Immediately after the Duchess and the Princess had entered they appeared at a window in the front of the hotel. While the royal party were at dinner, a band of musicians, stationed opposite the hotel in the Mall Green, played a number of popular airs, and in the evening a display of fireworks took place.

The next morning, Princess Victoria's mother met the Mayor of Bristol at the Council House and afterwards, with her daughter, was driven around Clifton Downs before returning to London after a short visit to Bath.

Queen Victoria's second visit was in 1899 when she knighted Councillor Ashman, as described above.

10

A TIME FOR CELEBRATION

In the first few years of the twentieth century the people of Bristol had much to celebrate before the long dark years of war. On 17 May 1909 church bells rang out across the city and flags flew from public buildings celebrating the news that Bristol was to have its own university. The new place of learning would be able to confer degrees on its students. This had been made possible by the granting of a charter by King Edward VII at a meeting of the Privy Council.

The University of Bristol evolved from University College, which was established in 1876 in Park Row in the centre of the city with just two professors and five lecturers, offering courses on fifteen subjects. It was the first higher educational institution in England offering places to women on an equal basis as men.

There had been a campaign running in the city for some time to get a university for Bristol. One of the main people behind this was Rev. Dr John Percival (who was later appointed Bishop of Hereford), the headmaster of Clifton College when it opened in 1862. He was a backer of the public meetings and fund-raising 'to promote a School of Science and Literature for the West of England'.

At the turn of the nineteenth century just £30,000 in endowments and donations had been received. The fund-raising was given a major boost when George Wills of the tobacco family read a letter to members of the Colston Research Society at their annual dinner in 1908. The letter came from his father, Henry Overton Wills, who wrote, 'I have decided to promise £100,000 to the endowment of a University for Bristol and the West of England, provided a Charter be granted within two years from this date.'

The Wills' donation acted as seed corn for shortly afterwards further financial help came from various individuals. More money was raised within twenty-four hours than had been attracted during the previous three decades. The city council offered the proceeds of a penny rate – about £7,000 a year – on condition that a charter was granted. The campaigners did not have to wait very long for their dreams to be realised. It was just seventeen months after Henry Wills made his promise that Edward VII gave his approval to a charter.

Henry Overton Wills, who also founded the professorial chairs of Greek, mathematics and physics, was appointed the university's first chancellor. Since its foundation the university has only had nine chancellors to date, all notable people, including the 10th Duke of Beaufort and Winston Churchill, who was installed into the prestigious office a couple of weeks before Christmas 1929. Students approved the appointment of Churchill and after the installation ceremony they carried him shoulder high to a meeting of the students' union in the Victoria Rooms.

Churchill was Chancellor until his death in 1965 and is the longest to serve in the role. On his eightieth birthday Churchill was at the university to witness the completion of the Queen's Building, which houses part of its engineering department.

A distinctive feature of the university's academic dress is that all hoods are University Red. The second Vice-Chancellor, Sir Isambard Owen – a godson of Isambard Kingdom Brunel – is said to have chosen the colour in 1910 from a band of limestone in the Avon Gorge.

The university now has six academic faculties running more than 200 undergraduate courses for more than 23,000 students. It has announced a major expansion scheme with the building of a £300 million campus for 3,000 students on the site of a post office sorting depot that has been derelict for more than twenty years in the Temple Quarter. Temple Quarter is also home to Bristol's Enterprise Zone, which already boasts rapidly growing clusters of small and start-up businesses, particularly in the creative, digital and hi-tech sectors.

FLYING HIGH

Bristol can arguably be said to be the birthplace of Britain's aircraft industry. It was in 1910 that Bristolian Sir George White set up the first major aircraft factory in the country with his own money in a disused tramcar depot.

The first successful venture of his Bristol and Colonial Aircraft Company was the Bristol Boxkite biplane, of which eighty were built and sold. A replica is suspended from the ceiling of the entrance hall at Bristol Museum.

Word had spread that a Boxkite aircraft would be making a demonstration flight from Bristol's Downs in November 1910. Thousands of people gathered on this open space and packed surrounding streets waiting for the event. They were not disappointed. Over four consecutive days they witnessed a total of six flights. The aircraft was in the air over the Downs and the Avon Gorge for a total of thirty minutes.

During the First World War more than 3,000 Bristol Fighter planes were built at the aircraft factories in Filton and Brislington. This plane had three machine guns and could carry over 100kg of bombs. Women worked in these factories for the first time, replacing the men who were fighting in the war.

Sir George White's company changed its name to the most apt Bristol Aeroplane Company in 1920. In the 1940s the firm was building what at the time was the world's biggest aircraft; the Brabazon had a wingspan of 230ft. The village of Charlton had been destroyed so that an extended runway could be built at Filton. The giant airliner cost £12 million to build but no one wanted to buy it. Four years after its maiden flight in 1949 the government scrapped the aircraft.

White's firm later joined with several other aircraft manufacturers to form the British Aircraft Corporation. At one time more than 40,000 people worked in the aircraft industry at Filton, many of them helping to build Concorde, the world's first supersonic airliner.

'WHITE CITY' EXHIBITION

Arguably, no better site in Bristol could have been chosen for a major international exhibition than the beauty spot of Rownham Meadows beside the River Avon, offering views of the Avon Gorge and Clifton Suspension Bridge.

The organisers of the Bristol International Exhibition had ambitious ideas to promote the city, its achievements and its potential for overseas trade with the Empire, as well as showcasing its history. Part of the exhibition's 32-acre site was devoted to some of England's history, with replicas of Bristol Castle, a set of Tudor buildings that formed an exhibit called 'Shakespeare's England', and a mock-up of Sir Francis Drake's ship, *Revenge*. There was also an international pavilion, a trade fair, and dance and concert halls where local choirs and military bands performed. Entertainment was enhanced by a nightly pageant depicting scenes from Bristol's history performed by up to 2,000 volunteers. Remarkably, there was also enough room for a menagerie of performing animals.

The exhibition was officially opened on 28 May 1914 by the Lord Mayor of Bristol, Alderman Sir John Swaish, accompanied by the mayors of four other towns.

Despite all the excitement, the Bristol International Exhibition closed its doors rather suddenly – just eight days after a rather grand opening ceremony. They were quickly reopened after there had been an injection of fresh funding to keep the show on the road. However, the exhibition continued to struggle with lower than expected attendance figures. Several county court hearings dealing with the exhibition's financial affairs were held before the exhibition finally closed on 20 August – two months ahead of schedule.

The exhibition, which had been staged by commercial organisers, had been beset by financial problems right from the start of the event, and possibly even before that. Many of the timber-framed buildings housing the various exhibits were only erected shortly before the event began. Most of the temporary buildings were clad with white plasterboard, giving rise to the site's nickname of 'the White City'.

After the exhibition closed, Rownham Meadows was taken over by the British Army as barracks for soldiers from the Gloucestershire Regiment who were being trained to serve in the First World War.

Today there is nothing left on the site to remind anyone of this unusual chapter in Bristol's history. Part of Rownham Meadows is now devoted to local people growing their own fruit and vegetables on a site called White City Allotments.

11

BRISTOL SIGNS UP

'BRISTOL'S OWN'

The first half of the twentieth century was dominated by two world wars. Many lives were lost in each war and the historic face of Bristol was changed for ever.

On Tuesday, 4 August 1914 Britain declared that it was at war with the German Empire. This was the day after a bank holiday when many families would have taken a day trip by charabanc or train to the nearby seaside towns of Weston-super-Mare, Clevedon and Portishead. This would be the last pleasure trip they would probably have for several years as public transport was needed to mobilise servicemen and transport their equipment and supplies around during the war.

The government launched a campaign to boost the number of soldiers in the British Army. To assist the War Office with its campaign, Alfred Leete, an artist and graphic designer from Weston-super-Mare, produced what became an iconic army recruiting poster. It depicted the newly appointed British Secretary of State for War, Lord Kitchener, wearing the cap of a British field marshal. He was staring straight ahead and pointing at anybody who looked at the poster, calling on them to enlist in the British Army against the Central Powers. Underneath Kitchener's portrait was the slogan 'Your Country Needs You'.

Kitchener wanted to recruit an extra 100,000 men to join those in the existing regular army. He sanctioned 'the enrolment of names of single men of the city of Bristol and neighbourhood between the ages of 19–35 who are willing to join the Colours for the duration of the war'. So many people wanted to serve King and country that a Bristol Citizens Recruiting Committee was formed. It set up an office at the Colston Hall and recruiting began on 15 August 1914 under the chairmanship of Sir Herbert Ashman, who had been the city's first Lord Mayor. Six weeks later the *Western Daily Press* noted that:

> for some weeks since the outbreak of war at the beginning of August he (Sir Herbert Ashman) had thrown himself with great energy into the task of recruiting men for the Forces and day after day he had been at the Colston Hall as Chairman of the Recruiting Committee which met daily.

Alfred Leete's poster seems to have had a dramatic effect in Bristol, for within a month more than 1,000 men, from teenagers upwards, were interviewed for potential Army service. Those who were accepted as fit and healthy to fight underwent training in Bristol before departing for France towards the end of 1915.

The city, showing a streak of independence, raised its own regiment that quickly became known by the local newspapers as 'Bristol's Own'. It was what was called a 'pals battalion' comprised of young men, some of whom were neighbours, friends and workmates. Some were motivated by patriotism and others wanted to see some action before it all ended, thinking they would be back home in time to spend Christmas with their families.

'Bristol's Own' was officially the 12th Battalion Gloucestershire Regiment. The recruits were initially stationed at Ashton Meadows in various buildings known as White City, the site of the ill-fated Bristol International Exhibition. The site was used as Army barracks until 1919.

The men and officers of 'Bristol's Own' took part in all the major battles in Flanders, France, and Italy between 1915 and 1918, when their regiment was disbanded. During the war 'Bristol's Own' gained an impressive tally of twenty-two battle honours.

Bristol sent about 55,000 men – both regular soldiers and recruits – to fight on the Western Front. Unfortunately, about 6,000 men never saw their families again. Among the British soldiers killed on the first day of the Battle of the Somme was Fred Wood, a 19-year-old from Bristol. His body was never found. Many of those who were fortunate enough to return to the bosom of their families were seriously injured.

The British Army on the Western Front was led by Douglas Haig, a former student at Clifton College. He became a field marshal and as Commander-in-Chief of the British Army in France was responsible for planning the Somme offensive in 1916.

Meanwhile, Bristol-born Fabian Ware, who was rejected by the British Army as being too old for front-line service, still found himself playing a major role in the war. He was surprised to find that there was no official system for recording the names of those who died or for even marking their graves. Therefore he formed an organisation that would do just that.

By May 1917 the Imperial (now Commonwealth) War Graves Commission was established by Royal Charter. The Prince of Wales became the president and Ware was appointed its vice-chairman, a post he held until his retirement in 1948. Fabian Ware insisted that headstones of all the graves of men who lost their lives in battle should be of the same design, with no distinction of rank, race or creed.

Fortunately, Bristol was never attacked during the First World War, unlike other British towns and cities. Perhaps the citizens who ensured that all house lights and street lamps were extinguished at night to 'hide' the city from possible air attack were to thank for this. Elsewhere in Britain more than 1,413 people were killed and a further 4,822 injured.

'BRAVO BRISTOL'

Frederick Weatherly, a leading barrister in Bristol, did his bit to raise morale among the troops and their families by putting to good use his way with words. Weatherly, who was also an author and lyricist, was so moved by the number of men volunteering for war service that he wrote a patriotic recruiting song specially for the newly formed Bristol battalion. He gave it a stirring title, 'Bravo Bristol'.

Music to accompany Weatherly's verses was composed by Ivor Novello, a composer and entertainer, whose first big hit was the wartime song 'Keep the Homes Fires Burning'.

'Bravo Bristol' was sung at recruiting rallies and at a farewell concert at the Colson Hall in May 1915 when 'Bristol's Own' were getting ready to leave for the Western Front. Fees received from the sale of the sheet music for the song were earmarked for the Regimental Fund of the Bristol Battalion.

Weatherly was a prolific song writer, having written the lyrics for 3,000 popular songs. Among his biggest hits was the wartime song 'Roses of Picardy'. The title refers to an area of France that includes the Somme, the scene of some of the bloodiest battles in the war.

WOMEN AT WORK

The war brought about major changes in the social and domestic lives of women left back at home. At the time it was not the tradition in Bristol, as in many other towns and cities across the country, for married women to go out to work but with their men folk fighting in the trenches many important jobs needed filling. In Bristol women were taken on for the first time as conductresses, or 'clippies' as they were known, on the trams. Their job was to collect fares from passengers and in return issue a ticket they then clipped, thus preventing any further use of it. At the end of the war soldiers who had returned to Bristol wanted their jobs on the trams back. However, the women refused to give up working and in April 1920 about 2,000 people gathered outside the tram company's offices in support of the ex-servicemen. Some ugly scenes developed with about thirty trams being damaged. The 'clippies' lost their jobs but the tram company gave them £5 each.

The high demand for weapons meant that munitions factories became one of the largest single employers of women during 1918. More than 1,000 women and girls were recruited by the Ministry of Munitions to work at a specially built factory at Chittening near Avonmouth. Working under strictly secret conditions, their job was to fill shells with the deadly mustard gas that the Germans had introduced into the war, killing thousands of soldiers. The British government decided to fight back with like for like.

Mustard gas is a colourless, oily liquid that produces a vapour that can affect the skin and lungs of anyone in close contact with it. It can cause blistering and even a slow, painful death. Although production at Chittening was short-lived, many of the women suffered serious illnesses and several of them died. At the end of 1918 the factory's medical officer reported 1,400 illnesses among the women, with some of them suffering more than one disease. They were treated at the factory's on-site hospital. The hazardous nature of the gas also meant that people living at Avonmouth were warned not to pick blackberries from bushes within a mile of the factory. Ironically, the mustard gas from Chittening arrived in France less than two months before the Armistice.

Bristol made sure its sons who were in the war zones were not deprived of some of the luxuries of life back home. Typical was one of the city's biggest employers at the time, the chocolate makers J.S. Fry and Son. The firm, founded in Bristol, sent out millions of bars of confectionery to the soldiers, while the W.D. & H.O. Wills tobacco factories dispatched thousands of cigarettes to them each week. One of their brands, the Woodbine, introduced in 1888 and sold in packets of five, ten and twenty, became a favourite with the troops. Both the Fry's and Wills factories employed large numbers of women.

HORSE POWER

Horses and mules played their part in the First World War, too. They were seen as a crucial form of transport, especially for moving munitions and supplies to the battlefronts. Horses and mules were regarded as being more reliable than military vehicles, which were liable to break down, especially as they were relatively new inventions.

Many of the horses taken to the front line had been requisitioned by the British Army from farms all over the country and even from family homes where they were treated as pets. Before being shipped to the war zones the animals were taken to what were known as Remount Depots. Here they would get several weeks of quarantine, be cleaned and checked by vets for any diseases and given some training.

One of the largest Remount Depots in the country was specially built at Shirehampton, then in the countryside just outside of Bristol. It was built on more than 100 acres of fields. Lord Kitchener, Secretary of State for War, approved the site because of its closeness to both rail links and the docks at Avonmouth, where horses were being brought into Remount Depots from as far away as Canada and America.

The first animals arrived at Shirehampton towards the end of 1914. The Remount Depot was large enough to stable up to 5,000 animals at a time. It is believed that during the war more than 300,000 horses passed through the Shirehampton site.

Veterinary hospitals in France treated more than 2½ million injured animals that were suffering from shell shock or battle wounds. Unfortunately, more than 8 million horses were said to have died in battle. At the end of the war surviving horses and mules were sold off to farmers in France. Those remaining at the Remount Depots in this country were auctioned off. The buildings at Shirehampton were dismantled in 1919 and there are no surviving signs to show that it ever existed.

12

POST-WAR BRISTOL

Soon after the end of the First World War, the council in Bristol became a large-scale house-builder. No doubt it was spurred on by the announcement from the government that it was granting subsidies to help local authorities build half a million homes across the country in three years.

Work started on four housing estates in different parts of the city – Hillfields in Fishponds, Sea Mills, Shirehampton and Knowle. The first houses to be completed were at Hillfields, where tenants started to occupy them in June 1920. Some of the properties had been built by men who had returned home from the war but were without permanent work.

Dr Christopher Addison, the Health and Housing Minister, launched the government's house-building programme at Sea Mills in June 1919. After the obligatory formal speeches and turf-cutting ceremony, the Lady Mayoress of Bristol planted an oak tree in commemoration of the event. It has become known as the 'Addison Oak'. Such was the importance of the occasion that after the tree planting a special organ recital was held at the Colston Hall.

Altogether 1,279 houses were built at Sea Mills, with seven to the acre, giving the occupants space and air around their homes. This was in vast contrast to many of the pre-war homes that had been built in tightly packed and airless courtyards in various parts of the city. They were, in effect, slums. The conditions in which people then lived led to an increasing number of health problems. In his speech Dr Addison said that he hoped other cities would follow the Sea Mills example.

Most of the homes at Sea Mills were built with three bed-rooms, a bathroom, a living room and a scullery. The first families arrived on the estate in August 1920 and many of them stayed there for the rest of their lives.

The day after the tree-planting the local morning news-paper, the *Western Daily Press*, ran a report headed 'Bristol's Housing Scheme – First Garden City Started'.

John Betjeman, who later became Poet Laureate but at the time was taking part in architectural programmes at the BBC's Bristol studios, described the Sea Mills development, which was close to the River Avon, as a 'Magic estate'.

BUILDING A TOWER

A principal post-war event for Bristol was that of King George V and Queen Mary officially opening the neo-Gothic 215ft-high Wills Memorial Building in June 1925. The tower, which stands sentinel-like over the centre of Bristol, is the jewel in the crown of the University of Bristol's campus.

It was built by the brothers Sir George and Henry Herbert Wills, as a monument to their father, Henry Overton Wills, who endowed the university in 1909 with the sum of £100,000.

Construction work on the tower began in 1914 but was interrupted by the First World War and not completed until 1925 at a cost of £501,566. Housed in the octagonal tower of the building is Great George, the country's seventh largest bell, which weighs in at 9.5 tonnes. It was cast at a foundry in Loughborough and was so big that two lorries were needed to transport it to Bristol. When Great George arrived after a twenty-four-hour journey it took another sixteen hours to lift it into position. The bell sounds the hour and is only manually swung on special occasions like the centenary birthday of the late Queen Mother and again on the death of Diana, Princess of Wales in 1997.

The Wills Memorial Building, which has more than fifty rooms, was designed by the eminent architect Sir George Oatley. Apparently his design was inspired by a dream in which he saw a tower standing on a hill adorned by shields all around it. Once he got down to his drawing board, Oatley took just three weeks to come up with the full plans and that was working at nights only. Nine shields on the sides of the tower represent well-known Bristol families including, of course, the Wills family.

The official opening of the Wills Memorial Building was a memorable occasion for the many thousands of people who lined the streets to watch the King and Queen arrive in their horse-drawn carriage. Not only were pavements lined with crowds five or six deep but first-floor balconies of shops and houses were packed, too. To officially open the doors of the Wills Memorial Building the King was given an extraordinarily large key. A local newspaper reported the King as saying that the occasion was 'very success-ful' although the weather had been 'very hot'. The Queen remarked that everything had gone off 'splendidly'.

'WE WILL REMEMBER THEM'

While most towns, cities and villages across the country unveiled their war memorials a couple of years or so after the end of hostilities, Bristolians had to wait more than a decade for their civic monument to appear.

Although a War Memorial Committee headed by the Lord Mayor of Bristol was formed soon after the Armistice, little progress was made for years. There were seemingly endless arguments among the committee members. Some of them preferred a purely commemorative structure and others wanted to see something more practical being built such as a memorial hospital. There were also debates about the cost and even the location of any memorial. Eventually, a competition among architects was held to find a suitable design.

So it was that thirteen years after the war had ended, Field Marshal Sir William Birdwood, an 'old boy' of Clifton College, found himself on a sunny June day in 1932 unveiling Bristol's civic war memorial. This was the Cenotaph at Colston Avenue in the centre of the city. Its design was similar to that of the Cenotaph in Whitehall.

The *Bristol Evening Post* reported that, 'There was less of the sense of poignancy of grief, rather a sense of satisfaction that at last there was a permanent memorial to the 6,000 gallant men and some few no less gallant women of Bristol who lived worthy of the traditions of their city and country even unto death.'

The ceremony was watched by an estimated crowd of 50,000 men, women and children. Not only did they pack the streets surrounding the Cenotaph but they filled every office window overlooking the memorial and even stood on the roofs of buildings. Those with a head for heights gathered on the top of the tower of nearby St Stephen's church.

Uniformed military service units lined up facing the Cenotaph. The singing of Rudyard Kipling's *Recessional* preceded the unveiling ceremony. Field Marshal Birdwood, in khaki uniform with his breast covered with four decks of service ribbons, then stepped forward.

As he pulled the cords that freed the shrouds covering the Cenotaph, a simple inscription of the dates of the start and end of the First World War , 1914–1918,was revealed. The dates of the Second World War were added after the end of those hostilities.

The *Bristol Evening Post* told its readers that the unveiling ceremony was part of a short service in which clergy from various religious denominations took part. Sir William Birdwood addressed the gathering, saying, 'It was the spirit of sacrifice which animated those Bristol citizens, officers and men, to pay the supreme price for which the memorial has been erected.'

Today the Cenotaph is regarded as commemorating the many people who have lost their lives in various conflicts, and not just the two World Wars. Every Remembrance Sunday since 1932 church and civic leaders, military units and thousands of citizens have gathered around the Cenotaph for a formal service of Remembrance led by local church leaders.

Bristol was one of the last of the major cities in Great Britain to unveil its civic memorial to the war dead.

What must have been the city's biggest memorial was unveiled in July 1921. This was a 6-acre plot of land at Horfield that officially became known as the Memorial Ground. It commemorated the lives of around 300 local rugby players who fell in the First World War. The cost of purchasing and equipping the ground as a rugby stadium was met through a public subscription fund. It became the home of Bristol Rugby Club for nearly eighty years.

13

A TOWN IN THE WEST

The loss of millions of military and civilian lives across the globe in the First World War and the huge amount of destruction caused led many people to believe this was the war to end all wars. But after two decades of peace on 1 September 1939 Germany invaded Poland and two days later Britain and France declared war on Germany, thus the Second World War had begun. The Luftwaffe (German Air Force) staged a blitz on Britain with a campaign of air raids. The word 'Blitz' came from the German Blitzkrieg, meaning 'lightning war'.

With aircraft factories on the northern fringe of the city, Avonmouth Docks to the west and the city docks right in the middle of town, Bristol was a prime target for enemy action during the war.

Bristol's citizens first heard the wailing sound of air raid sirens warning of an imminent attack shortly after midnight on 25 June 1940. It was heard for the last time on 13 June 1944. Throughout the war years there were a total of seventy-seven air raids on the city, with all the major attacks occurring during the early part of the war. At the end of the war, members of Bristol's Air Raid Precautions Committee were given the grim details of the toll on both human life and buildings. They heard that 1,299 people lost their lives, and a further 3,505 were injured. It seems that air raids were classed as major blitzes only if at least 100 people were killed. More than 3,000 homes were destroyed and a further 100,000 properties damaged. Some 20,000 children were evacuated from their homes or boarding schools to Somerset, Devon and Cornwall for safety reasons. It was not a wasted move for Bristol turned out to be the fifth most heavily bombed city in the country.

A memorial to the civilians – men, women and children – who were killed is fixed to the blitzed ruins of St Peter's church on Castle Park. It takes the form of a plaque bearing their names. Some of the victims were firemen, air raid wardens and police officers.

BRISTOL WIPED OUT

In the first major air raid, which came on the night of Sunday, 24 November 1940, German bombers wrought havoc upon Bristol and its citizens. Many lives were lost that night and the historic face of Bristol was changed for ever. Nearly 150 planes of the German Air Force were tasked with 'eliminating Bristol as an importing port supplying much of the Midlands and South of England'.

The raid started at about 6.30 p.m., with the 'all clear' siren being sounded at midnight. During those five-and-a-half hours the heart of the city was reduced to twisted girders, ashes and rubble. The whole of the area known as Castle Park, once the site of the city's Noman castle, was destroyed. The city's main shopping centre, with many national stores represented there, was no more. Two churches on Castle Park, St Mary le Port and St Peter's, were bombed. The ruins of these buildings still stand as a reminder of the devastation that war can cause. What remains of St Mary le Port, believed to have been founded in Saxon times, is now surrounded by office buildings that date back to the 1960s. The ruins of St Mary le Port are important as this was one of five ancient churches in the city. At the beginning of 2020 the church was on Historic England's Heritage at Risk Register.

A few hundred yards away the remaining four walls and tower of St Peter's church can be clearly seen. Stand beside the tower and you can almost hear the congregation singing the final hymn before the vicar cut short the Sunday evening service. He had heard an air raid siren giving warning of an imminent raid and sent the worshippers home.

Temple Church was also destroyed but its landmark leaning tower escaped damage. The story is often related by Bristolians who lived through the Second World War that a soldier had to be dissuaded from demolishing the tower for safety reasons, believing that enemy action had made it a dangerous building. However, during construction in the fourteenth century the foundations of the 113ft-high tower subsided. Although attempts were made to throw the tower back they were unsuccessful and ever since Bristol's answer to the Leaning Tower of Pisa has stood at 5ft out of true.

Bristol Cathedral narrowly escaped heavy bombs, although much ancient glass was destroyed.

It wasn't just the centre of Bristol that was heavily bombed that night. Bombs also fell on other parts of the city, including College Green and Clifton. Many public and historic buildings, including more than twenty churches, were extensively damaged, some beyond repair, while others were immediately lost forever. At Bristol University, the Great Hall in the Wills Memorial Building, used for degree congregations and other ceremonial events, was wrecked. The museum was a total loss and the city's Art Gallery was badly damaged.

Alderman Thomas Underdown, the Lord Mayor of Bristol, later wrote:

> As darkness fell the alert was given and by 6.30 the skies over the centre of the city were brightly lit by flares dropped by enemy planes. Then the fiery attack was let loose with utter ruthlessness. High Explosive bombs whistled and screamed to earth. The flames of buildings on fire appeared as one huge fiery furnace leaping into the air and giving an intensity of daylight over a great part of the city.

He went on: 'The city of churches had in one night become the city of ruins.'

The Germans were quite pithy about what happened that night, saying that they had 'wiped out Bruder'. This was the enemy's wartime code name for Bristol.

The statistics of that first major raid make shocking reading, even more than seventy years on. More than 5,000 incendiaries and 10,000 high explosive bombs were dropped. More than 200 people lost their lives and nearly 700 more were injured. Ten thousand homes were damaged or destroyed. So many fires broke out in the ruins that the local fire brigade had to be reinforced by dozens of brigades from neighbouring counties, with an extra 20,000ft of those also coming from Cardiff, Newport, Bournemouth and Plymouth.

After most of the air raids there were grim stories for the local newspapers to report both in terms of the number of lives lost and the damage caused. As security was of the utmost importance, newspaper reports of air raids did not identify exactly where bombs had fallen. Headlines frequently referred to a 'Town in the West'.

In one day-light raid on an aircraft factory at Filton, more than ninety men were killed. Some of them had sought safety in the air raid shelters but to no avail.

During a twelve-hour-long air raid in January 1941, the Luftwaffe dropped its biggest bomb on Bristol. It was more than 8ft long with a diameter of 2ft 2in and weighed 4,400lb. The bomb landed in the road fronting a terrace of houses in the Knowle district of the city, with local people giving it the nickname of 'Satan'. Specially trained soldiers made the bomb safe and recovered it from the 29ft-deep crater it had created in the road. The bomb was given a place of honour in the post-war Victory Parade in London.

On Good Friday 1941, a bomb hit a tramline on Redcliffe Hill with such force that a piece of rail was hurled several hundred yards over the rooftops of shops and homes, eventually embedding itself in the churchyard of St Mary Redcliffe. It still stands there at a precarious angle. The vicar of Redcliffe at the time said that the piece of rail was a reminder of the 'horrors of war'. Fortunately, this historic church itself survived the attacks on Bristol even though its spire, just shy of 300ft above street level, would have been a target for enemy aircraft. The vicar of Redcliffe could often be seen on the church roofs leading teams of volunteer fire-watchers who were clearing gutters and removing any incendiaries.

Hardly a hymn book's throw from St Mary Redcliffe stands St Paul's church, Southville, which received a direct hit that same night. Only its tower and four walls were left standing. Remarkably, 300 people who had sought refuge in the crypt were unhurt. Some of them described this as a 'modern miracle'. The nearby daughter church of St David became the temporary parish church for seventeen years until rebuilding of St Paul's was completed.

The city's tram service came to an abrupt end after carrying passengers for nearly fifty years when a bomb hit a bridge in St Phillips next to a generating centre. It cut the power supply to the trams. On 28 August 1942, a bomb

St Paul's church, Southville

was dropped on Broad Weir where three buses picking up passengers immediately caught alight. Forty-five people were killed and a further fifty-six were injured.

So many people were killed in the numerous air raids that there were often communal burials at Greenbank cemetery.

One hundred and twenty-nine victims of the bombing lie at rest there.

A 'LOCAL FRACAS'

Park Street, the steep hill rising up from the city centre to Clifton, was once known as Bristol's answer to London's Bond Street. This was on account of its elegant stores selling designer fashions, luxury goods, fine jewellery and exclusive brands.

It was on the corner of Great George Street and Park Street that ugly racial scenes erupted one Saturday evening in July 1944 as more than 400 black and white American soldiers fought with each other. Around 120 Military Police officers, all of whom were white, intervened. In a bid to contain the situation they blocked nearby streets by getting buses to park across them.

As the black soldiers were being escorted back to their camps, one Military Police officer was stabbed in the leg. Some shooting followed with several black soldiers being injured, one of whom died later. Others were taken to Bristol Royal Infirmary for treatment.

Despite the large number of people involved in the fighting, it was dismissed by the *Bristol Evening Post* with a short news report that was simply headlined 'Local Fracas'. A sub-heading read 'People injured in Bristol'. The five-paragraph report across a single column at the bottom of the front page did not say exactly where the incident happened or that it involved black and white American soldiers.

During the war large numbers of American servicemen were drafted into Britain. Many of them were stationed in Bristol, with camps for them being set up in various suburbs of the city as well as in the north Somerset villages of Flax

Bourton, Brockley, Failand, Nailsea and Backwell, all of which were very close to Bristol. Some of the soldiers were billeted in private homes in the leafy north-west Bristol suburbs of Westbury on Trym, Shirehampton and Henleaze. Many Bristolians had sympathy with the African-American soldiers and were friendly with them.

The soldiers were racially segregated, which was official practice in the United States forces. Although the British government did not agree with this, it did not interfere with the situation while the American troops were on British soil. Segregation was also imposed on the leisure time enjoyed by the soldiers. The rather elegant Royal West of England Academy building on Queen's Road, Clifton, for example, became a club for white GIs. The black troops could use the nearby Red Cross Club on Great George Street, a much smaller building. The black soldiers became resentful at being prevented from using what they saw as the best pubs and clubs in the city.

BOOSTING BRISTOL'S MORALE

During the war many distinguished people visited Bristol, not only to see for themselves the devastation caused by bombing but also to help boost the morale of citizens. Among the first visitors were King George VI and Queen Mary, who walked among the ruins two weeks before Christmas 1940.

The Prime Minister, Sir Winston Churchill, was in the city in April 1941 on the morning after the so-called 'Good Friday Raid'. Although he was there in his role as Chancellor of Bristol University he found time to visit suburbs that were bombed the night before. At the university, Sir Winston was due to confer honorary degrees on John

Gilbert Winant, the American Ambassador to Britain, and Robert Gordon Menzies, Prime Minister of Australia. The ceremony was due to take place in the university's Great Hall but it had been extensively damaged by bombing. The Prime Minister brushed aside the smouldering rubble and insisted the ceremony should still go ahead, albeit in another room that remarkably had escaped damage.

Afterwards, while Sir Winston and his wife were seeing for themselves bomb damage in Southville, an elderly woman called out to him to stop the war. Newspapers later reported his reply: 'We'll give it them back.'

Queen Mary, the widow of George V, who had moved out of London to stay with the Duke of Beaufort's family at Badminton House, South Gloucestershire, throughout the war made frequent visits to Bristol, although they were not normally made known to the public in advance. Queen Mary made a private visit to St Mary Redcliffe church shortly after the outbreak of the war and was shown around by the vicar and churchwardens. On another visit she was taking Holy Communion while a young couple were waiting to be married. The bridegroom was called up for war service immediately after the ceremony.

On other occasions Queen Mary visited the Royal Hospital for Sick Children, where she met medical and nursing staff along with some of the patients. On a visit to Clifton College she watched American troops who were based there, helping to plan the D-Day operation, playing a game of baseball.

AN EXTRAORDINARY 'RELATIONSHIP' WITH AMERICA

Bristol had its very own wartime 'special relationship' with America but in a most unusual way. The city sent the United States a large amount of rubble from buildings that had been bombed. This rather strange cargo crossed the Atlantic Ocean as ballast in ships that had brought to England much-needed supplies, including food, but were returning home empty.

In New York the rubble was used in creating the foundations of Bristol Basin in Manhattan. A plaque commemorating this unusual link between Bristol and New York City was unveiled at a ceremony in June 1942 organised by the English Speaking Union. Part of the inscription on the plaque reads:

> These fragments that once were homes shall testify while men love freedom to the resolution and fortitude of the people of Britain ... They saw their homes struck down without warning. It was not their homes but their valour that kept them free.

The plaque remained in place until 1970 when the area was redeveloped. Construction work was completed four years later when the Bristol-born Hollywood film star Cary Grant rededicated the plaque.

More of Bristol's wartime rubble was put to use much nearer to home in the reclamation of land at Avonmouth Docks. Some 30 acres of rubble formed the foundations of a new sea terminal for petroleum tankers.

BUILDING THE 'NEW BRISTOL'

With almost 3,000 homes destroyed across the city, nearly 100,000 properties damaged and a shopping centre totally demolished, Bristol's planners lost no time in taking on the massive task of designing a 'new Bristol'. Beaten but not bowed, they set about drawing up plans for the present shopping centre at Broadmead with arcaded shops, a central bus station nearby and new arterial roads. After a long spell as city council-run surface car parks, the site that was once home to Bristol Castle and later a shopping centre was unveiled in 1978 as Castle Park, a large public park.

Immediately after the war the government launched a major programme of council-house building. Aircraft firms around the country, including the Bristol Aircraft Company, set about building prefabricated aluminium housing in kit form. Some of the aluminium had been salvaged from crashed aircraft. Pre-fabricated homes were seen as a way of quickly increasing the country's housing stock. The very first prefabricated home to be erected and occupied in the country was at Shirehampton in 1945.

The prefabs were meant to last for only ten years but in Bristol families loved them so much that they were still being occupied some sixty years later. Their end finally came when the city council completed a ten-year scheme in 2014 with new homes for those living in prefabs. It is estimated that a total of 156,622 prefabs were erected both locally and nationally in the four years after the war, with around 2,700 being built in Bristol.

THE 'FUN FACTORY'

During the Second World War the BBC moved its major departments including light entertainment, religious affairs, schools and children's programmes along with the BBC Symphony Orchestra to Bristol in case Broadcasting House in London was attacked by enemy action.

By 1940 six studios were set up at Broadcasting House in Clifton, which had been opened six years earlier. One of the first broadcasters from the Bristol studios was John Betjeman, who had been booked to give talks about architecture. He later became better known as a poet who became Poet Laureate. Betjeman once described the studio buildings – a grand villa on a corner of Whiteladies Road – as 'rather like a dentist's house in a provincial town'.

With the influx of staff from London the number of BBC employees in Bristol soared from under fifty to nearly 1,000. It meant that more large houses in Clifton had to be acquired and converted into studios. Nearby church halls were also taken over and adapted for use. As the number of variety programmes made in Bristol increased, staff affectionately nicknamed the studios 'the Fun Factory'.

With the fall of France in the early part of the war, Bristol was considered to be within bombing range of the German Luftwaffe. This prompted the BBC to move some of its studios further west into Wales and also into a tunnel in the defunct Clifton Rocks Railway that had been built in the rocks of the Avon Gorge.

The tunnel was converted by BBC engineers into a studio complex that included recording and transmitter rooms alongside a studio equipped for music and drama productions. To make sure acoustics in the tunnel were just right for broadcasting, the full BBC Symphony Orchestra, nearly 100 musicians in all, was brought in to play under the baton of conductor Sir Adrian Boult.

Engineers also installed a piece of equipment that probably would not be needed in any other studio in the land; this was an ozonator, which was needed to oxidise airborne odours from the smell of the River Avon close by. If Broadcasting House in London was attacked, the BBC could easily switch to broadcasting from Bristol even if an announcer was part way through reading a national news bulletin.

The corporation had a lease on the Clifton Rocks tunnel with rent fixed at 1s a year for twenty-one years. The transmitter in the tunnel was used as a booster station until 1960, when the BBC finally moved out its equipment.

14

THE 1960s TO THE 1990s

The so-called 'Swinging Sixties' well and truly arrived in Bristol when in 1966 the Mecca organisation opened the ballroom of its £2 million New Bristol Centre, which included banqueting suites, bowling lanes, a casino, bingo hall and cinema. The ballroom alone had room for 2,000 people and hosted everything from the BBC's *Come Dancing* programmes to concerts featuring some of the top pop stars of the day, including The Who, well known for smashing up their guitars and drums on stage.

A couple of hundred yards along the road from the new entertainments centre, the much older Colston Hall was regularly staging several pop concerts a week. 'Sold out' notices appeared on the three occasions the Beatles, or the 'Fab Four' as the group was dubbed by newspapers and fans, took to the Colston Hall stage. There were dramatic scenes when the Beatles made their final appearance in Bristol in 1964. While they were playing 'If I Fell', several practical jokers who had found their way into the loft of the concert hall, despite tight security, dropped a bag of flour on to the stage 50ft below. The Beatles, covered in white flour, simply laughed and played on.

It seemed that every youngster in the city had dreams of reaching the Number One spot in the record charts by forming their own pop group. Local showbiz manager John Miles had his work cut out with handling the bookings for more than 300 groups from his one-room office in Clifton. Many of the bands were working full time at clubs in Germany.

At the same time, John Miles introduced the nation to a local group with the name Adge Cutler and the Wurzels. Adge (his real name was Alan John) wrote and sang songs about Somerset villages and Somerset cider, accompanied by his folk band. Hence the group quickly became known as 'Scrumpy and Western' musicians. The band eventually reached the top of the charts with a number entitled 'Combine Harvester'. Sadly, Adge could not enjoy that success, having died two years earlier aged 44. He was killed in a car crash while driving home after playing in a concert in Hereford.

The 1960s also saw the brothers Frank and Aldo Berni change the nation's eating habits and encourage people to dine out. Their Bristol-based pub restaurant chain Berni Inns offered a simple menu of prawn cocktail, steak and chips followed by Black Forest gateau. Having started their business in a cellar bar in the middle of Bristol, the brothers went on to open more than 150 branches all over the country. They eventually sold their empire for £14.5 million.

BUS BOYCOTT

In the spring of 1963 a campaign calling on the people of Bristol to boycott the city's bus service was launched because the state-owned but locally run Bristol Omnibus Company refused to employ non-white people as conductors or drivers.

The company operated the ban although Bristol had an estimated 3,000 residents of West Indian origin, some of whom had served in the British military during the Second World War. Others arrived in Britain after the war with some of them settling in Bristol, where they formed a tightly knit community in the St Paul's district.

The boycott was led by youth worker Paul Stephenson and the West Indian Development Council. Stephenson, the son of an African father and a white British mother, was motivated by racial injustice and the inspiration of the US civil rights movement. Some of those helping with the organisation of the campaign would have been descendants of victims of the slave trade.

The campaign was supported by high-profile national politicians, including the Labour Party leader Harold Wilson who was elected Prime Minister the following year. He told an anti-apartheid rally in London that he was 'glad that so many Bristolians are supporting the [boycott] campaign ... we wish them every success'. Interventions were also made by church groups and the High Commissioner for Trinidad and Tobago, Sir Learie Constantine, the ex-West Indies cricketer, who condemned the bus company. So too did diplomats from Jamaica and other Caribbean territories.

Four months to the day after the boycott was announced, the bus company dropped its colour bar. By mid-September Bristol had its first non-white bus conductor, Raghbir Singh, an Indian-born Sikh who had lived in the city since 1959. On his first day working for the bus company he told the *Western Daily Press* he would wear a blue turban to work because it 'goes with my uniform'.

It is thought that the campaign played a major part in getting Parliament to pass the Race Relations Act in 1965. The Act made 'racial discrimination unlawful in a public place'. The Race Relations Act 1968 extended the provisions of the earlier Act to employment and housing.

The Great Flood

Eight lives were lost in Bristol and the West Country in July 1968 when 5in of rain, accompanied by thunder and lightning, swamped the area in twenty-four hours. It was said to have been the worst storm in the region for more than fifty years. National newspapers lost no time in calling it 'The Great Flood'.

At the height of the storm, Bristol City Council was receiving telephone calls for help from householders at the rate of one every fifteen seconds. One man reported that a tree trunk had come into his home through a skylight in the roof.

Emergency accommodation had to be found for hundreds of families in south Bristol, the worst-hit part of the city. In many cases floodwater had reached bedroom level of houses and families were rescued by rowing boats. The freak storm brought production at many firms to a standstill. At the W.D. & H.O. Wills tobacco factories in Bedminster and Ashton, some 50 million cigarettes along with 210,000 tons of tobacco ready for distribution to shopkeepers had to be dumped on a refuse tip at Lawrence Weston in the north-west of the city. The next day Bristol featured on the front pages of national newspapers. Scavengers were photographed salvaging cigarettes and condemned food from the refuse tip despite warnings of the danger to health. As packets of twenty cigarettes exchanged hands for a shilling, diesel oil was sprayed over the tip to discourage further salvaging. The police had every available officer on the site but confessed they were powerless to stop the scavengers as there were so many of them.

Centuries-old stone bridges in villages just outside Bristol collapsed in the storm. Royal Engineers were called in to erect temporary Bailey bridges. The Duke of Edinburgh arrived by helicopter to see for himself the devastation and to raise morale among some of the many flood victims.

A police report following an investigation into what caused the flooding said that initially the fall of rain was heavy but not out of the ordinary, but within a few hours it had escalated into a 'terrifying thunderstorm' that struck without warning. The storm was officially classified by the Meteorological Office as 'remarkable' and 'very rare'.

UP, UP AND AWAY

In April 1969 thousands of people, including several hundred journalists, film crews, radio and television reporters from across the world, descended on Filton on the northern edge of Bristol. The occasion was to witness history in the making as Concorde 002, the world's first supersonic airliner, made its maiden flight. Spectators started to arrive at Filton early in the morning, searching for what they hoped would be the best viewing point. Some families camped out on a nearby golf course. The A38 trunk road passing the runway was closed to traffic and taken over by a sea of spectators. The roofs of the aircraft factory where Concorde 002 was built provided scores of workers with a grandstand view.

It was not only Concorde that was using Filton airfield on 9 April; aircraft were also flying in from Toulouse carrying politicians along with officials and engineers from Sud Aviation, the French state-owned aircraft manufacturer that was working with the British Aircraft Corporation on the supersonic project. Between them the two aircraft companies had invited more than 1,000 guests.

Although the French Concorde 001 had made its maiden flight a month earlier, there was still tremendous excitement and tension among the ever-growing crowd of onlookers. The hours of waiting ended as the British Aircraft Corporation's chief test pilot Brian Trubshaw started up the plane's mighty Olympus engines. At 2.24 p.m. silence fell over the crowds as Concorde taxied to the end of the runway. After last-minute cockpit checks by the crew, Concorde streaked down the runway and climbed into the air with a reverberating roar from its engines. This was accompanied by loud cheering and sustained applause from the watching crowds.

Concorde made a subsonic flight lasting just twenty-two minutes before landing at RAF Fairford, 50 miles to the east in Gloucestershire. Trubshaw and his crew emerged triumphant from a successful first flight. Before going into to a debriefing, the pilot told the waiting press corps that the flight had gone according to plan. 'It was wizard – really beautiful and the whole flight was exceptionally smooth. We were cool, calm and collected.'

A total of just twenty Concorde aircraft – six for development purposes and the others for commercial service – were built by the British and French governments. During their flying careers the planes carried 2½ million passengers across the Atlantic Ocean and to other parts of the world. Britain and France had hoped to take the world by storm by selling 400 aircraft. However, various factors including rising oil costs and environmental lobbying in the USA affected the programme and Concorde was eventually retired in 2003 following a crash three years earlier.

Concorde 002 is now at the Fleet Air Arm Museum, Yeovilton, while Concorde 216 – the last of the fleet to fly – is a popular attraction at the Bristol Aerospace Museum at Filton. It was retired to the museum after a farewell flight in 2003 from Heathrow to Filton, when it flew at low level across Bristol as a tribute to the many thousands of Bristolians who had worked on the plane.

The public's interest in the Concorde project has never waned. There was a rush for tickets when the BBC transmitted an edition of *Antiques Roadshow* and a live Radio 4 broadcast of *Any Questions?* from the Bristol Aerospace Museum in 2019. The programmes were part of the celebrations to mark the fiftieth anniversary of Concorde's maiden flight.

SHE'S HOME AT LAST

Around 100,000 people lined both sides of the River Avon as the rusting hulk of Isambard Kingdom Brunel's SS *Great Britain* was returning to its original berth to be restored.

As the ship slid majestically under Brunel's Clifton Suspension Bridge for the first time – the bridge had not been completed when the SS *Great Britain* made its maiden voyage in 1843 – well-wishers waved flags and cheered loudly and almost endlessly. Spectators standing on the bridge rained confetti and flower petals on to the ship. In the search for the best viewing points, some people perched precariously on the rocks of the Avon Gorge.

When the SS *Great Britain* arrived at Avonmouth Docks, cracks in its hull were repaired and the ship floated off the giant pontoon on which it had been carried from the Falkland Islands. The ship was floated up the River Avon into Bristol on its own hull being pulled by tugs and accompanied by an armada of small vessels.

The SS *Great Britain* was eventually inched into the dry dock on 19 July 1970, exactly 127 years to the day after she was floated out into Bristol Docks for the first time. The ship was now being nudged into her berth by two tugs, a heave by a couple of bulldozers and a shove from the Lord Mayor of Bristol and thirty other distinguished guests. The hull had to be exactly placed to settle the keel on a cradle of elm wood blocks that would support the ship when the dock was drained.

On board for part of the last leg of the ship's journey home was the Duke of Edinburgh. He walked around the SS *Great Britain* on specially constructed catwalks. The ship's welcoming committee at the docks included Jack Hayward, a millionaire businessman who had made the ship's salvage operation possible with a donation of £150,000.

A multi-million pound restoration project quickly got under way and the SS *Great Britain* is now a major tourist attraction, winning many national, heritage, conservation and educational awards.

600 YEARS A COUNTY

The year 1973 was something of a milestone in Bristol's history. It was the sixth centenary of the granting by King Edward III of a charter that made Bristol a county in its own right with special judicial privileges. No one who was in Bristol, no matter how fleeting their visit, in the anniversary year left unaware that it was celebrating in grand style.

Dominating the gardens in the centre of the city and standing 20ft above the ground was a specially made charter crown festooned with garlands of lights. Thirty-two flagpoles around the edge of the gardens commemorated the number of monarchs since Edward III. Elegant Georgian squares were decorated with hanging baskets of flowers and charter banners fluttered in the wind from every conceivable high point around the dockside.

It was ironic that in less than a year's time county status would be taken away from Bristol. No one though was thinking about that as festival fever gripped the town. The highlight of the county celebrations was the three-week

Evening Post Bristol 600 Exhibition, staged by the local newspaper on 60 acres of Clifton and Durdham Downs. The editor of the paper described it as 'an exhibition of a magnitude never before attempted in Bristol'. The exhibition was housed 'in the largest marquee system in Europe'.

There were pavilions dedicated to 600 years of local history, Bristol's trade, its role in shipping and aviation, its people, and its newspaper history, which dates back to 1702. A medieval fayre, staged by a Bristol restaurant firm, included nightly jousting tournaments with mounted and armoured knights from the British Jousting Society. While battle between the knights ensued, guests wearing period costume sat down to a medieval-style banquet. As a nod to the times, a Miss Bristol 600 competition was held with twelve girls in the final round competing for the winner's crown.

The last week of the exhibition included the actual anniversary of the signing of the charter on 8 August 1373. Among the many thousands of visitors that week was the Queen, although her tour of the show site had to be cut short following thirty-six hours of rain and gales. Many marquees had been brought to the ground during the prolonged storm, which turned large areas of the showground site into a quagmire. The Queen made a short tour of the site standing behind the cab of an open-back vehicle.

Earlier in the day the Queen had visited the offices of the city council, which she officially opened in 1956, to see an exhibition of some of the many charters that her predecessors had granted to Bristol.

AVON CALLING

The 1970s saw the start of a completely reorganised system of local government. This followed a Royal Commission that looked at the administration of counties all over the country.

An Act of Parliament meant that on 1 April 1974 Bristol lost its county status and all the civic pageantry and traditions that went with the honour. Instead it became a local government district of a newly formed county with the uninspiring name of Avon. Presumably it was inspired by the name of the river that flows through the area.

The legal draughtsmen responsible for the wording of the Act had disregarded King Edward III's charter, which stipulated that Bristol should be its own county 'forever'. Instead, Bristol was transferred, along with parts of the neighbouring counties of Somerset and Gloucestershire, into the newly formed Avon County.

Many citizens made it clear that they did not like losing county status one little bit and did not waste time in making their opinions known. Petitions opposing the boundary changes were arriving almost daily at Downing Street from disgruntled voters. National and local newspapers were filling their correspondence columns with anti-Avon letters. Banner-carrying protesters held rallies outside council offices. However, all their efforts turned out to be in vain.

As the clock struck midnight on 31 March 1974, an unusual ceremony saw the bittersweet way in which the outgoing Bristol City Council held its final meeting. A fanfare of trumpets – probably the only time such instruments have been played at a local authority meeting – marked the council's end, with the Lord Mayor's chain of office being removed from his shoulders. The historic office of alderman ceased at the same time; many men and women honoured with the title were saying a final farewell to their colleagues. A few minutes later, local government reorganisation became effective as Bristol City Council gave way to a meeting of its successor authority, the Bristol District Council.

The people of Avon had a permanent reminder that they were now living in a new county as the new council had taken over a speculatively built eighteen-storey office block in the centre of Bristol for its headquarters. They named it Avon House. A local vicar mourned the passing of Bristol's county status by flying a black flag over his home on 1 April every year.

However, the new county was to be short lived. Just over two decades later, in another round of local government boundary changes, Avon County was abolished by the government. On 1 April 1996, Bristol became a unitary authority and took back all of the traditions, civic ceremonies and pageantry it had lost. Although Avon County no longer exists, the name refuses to die. It survives in the titles of various institutions and businesses such as Avon and Somerset Police, Avon Coroner's Court, Avon and Somerset Fire and Rescue Service and Avon Wildlife Trust.

HISTORY REPEATS ITSELF

In the 1990s maritime history was recreated with the building of a replica of the explorer John Cabot's ship *The Matthew* in which he discovered Newfoundland. The replica was built by a dozen shipwrights using medieval tools in the Redcliffe Wharf part of the docks just beneath St Mary Redcliffe church. The ship would eventually recreate Cabot's 1497 voyage across the Atlantic Ocean.

The Duke of Edinburgh agreed to be patron of the project and laid the ship's keel in May 1994. About 18,000 people watched as *The Matthew* was launched a year later. A bottle of John Harvey's Bristol Cream sherry was used to launch *The Matthew* instead of the champagne that is traditional for such ceremonies.

The ship became a highlight at the Festival of the Sea in the Floating Harbour in 1996, after which she sailed to Ireland and France before returning to Bristol for the winter.

Five hundred years to the day after John Cabot set sail from Bristol, *The Matthew* was all set for the re-enactment of his epic voyage. A crew of local men attended a special service at St Mary Redcliffe, where the congregation prayed for their safety, just as Cabot had done. Then they stepped aboard *The Matthew.*

While Cabot had no one to greet him when he made landfall in 1497, this time the crew were met at Bonavista, Newfoundland, by the Queen and the Duke of Edinburgh, some 30,000 spectators and television cameras transmitting their pictures of the end of the voyage around the world.

15

MOVING INTO THE TWENTY-FIRST CENTURY

Bristol's glory days as a port in the very centre of the city are long gone. However, the City and County of Bristol has reinvented itself. No longer does it prosper from the vices of the wine, tobacco and slave trades. Gone, too, are the metal-bashing industries at one time to be found on almost every street corner. Gone, as well, are the factories where chocolate, cartons and packaging materials were made. Boots and shoes along with structural steelwork are no longer manufactured here.

Although Bristol dates back 1,000 years, it is not sleeping in the shadows of its ancient past. Not only has it become the largest city in the West of England but also effectively its capital. It is a prosperous, successful modern city thanks to an ongoing commercial and cultural revolution. Its modern economy is built on the creative media, electronics and aerospace industries, while the docks in the city centre have been redeveloped as centres of heritage and culture.

Computer keyboard tapping has replaced the industries of bygone years as Bristol thrives from a boom in the number of firms providing financial and legal services. Some of these firms have moved into the city from London.

Bristol is also benefiting from a burgeoning digital technology sector. Many start-up businesses are specialising in everything from robotics to indoor vertical farming, which uses cutting-edge technology to grow the farms of the future. Some 30,000 people are now estimated to be working in the local digital technology field.

THE HOLLYWOOD OF THE WEST COUNTRY

In the austere years after the Second World War, buddleia bushes blossomed for decade after decade on bombed sites where nothing else seemed to happen. No one could have imagined that one day Bristol would have its very own answer to the film studios of Hollywood. The Bottle Yard Studios with back-up services for film and programme producers is the largest dedicated film and television production space in the West Country. It is a partnership initiative with Bristol City Council that is housed in a building that was once home to the full production line for Harvey's Bristol Cream sherry, run by John Harvey and Sons, a family business founded in the city in 1796.

Bristol Film Office has played a big role in helping to make Bristol a centre for film makers. In 2017 the city was named a UNESCO Creative City of Film. It is not unusual to see the Georgian crescents and squares being turned into film sets for major costume dramas for both television and the big screen featuring actors with household names. Much of the popular television series *Poldark* was filmed at the Bottle Yard Studios. Some 15,000 people now work in the city's film and television industry. Since 2003 the industry's contribution to the local economy has been £235 million. In 2018–19 alone it contributed £16 million to the local economy, says the Film Office, with Bottle Yard Studios alone creating almost 500 jobs.

DOCKS REGENERATION

One of the most visible changes to Bristol's landscape that is also benefiting the local economy is the ongoing regeneration of the Floating Harbour or city docks. This has been transformed from a decayed area into a vibrant, prosperous part of the town based on leisure, tourism and waterfront living. No longer are the jibs of cranes dipping into ships' holds to unload cargoes on to the quayside. Old rotting and rusting transit sheds, derelict railway sidings overgrown with weeds, a flour mill, and even a disused gas works are among the many buildings and structures that have been either demolished or converted to make way for offices, thousands of apartments, restaurants and bars situated along both sides of the waterfront.

Large metal containers usually seen on ships' decks now line the quayside at Wapping Wharf, with some of them standing on top of one another in a new venture known as Cargo Yard. The containers have been given a new lease of life as independent shops, restaurants and cafes. Nearby, on the site of an old dry dock that later became a 1950s transit shed, is the M Shed Museum, which is all about Bristol.

Developers of Wapping Wharf are even incorporating the ruins of the grim and foreboding gateway of the nineteenth-century prison that overlooked the docks into their plans. It will become a central feature of a mixed residential and retail development.

COUNCIL CHANGE

In 2012 a big change came with the administration of the city. Bristol was one of eleven English cities to hold a referendum organised by the government to see if the electorate wanted a directly elected Mayor. The result of the referendum showed that Bristol was the only city to vote in favour of having such an officer added to the city council's payroll. Later that year fifteen candidates stood in an election for the post of directly elected Mayor. The office comes up for renewal at an election held every four years. The post should not be confused with that of the Lord Mayor of Bristol, which is largely ceremonial and non-political.

COUNTING HEADS

Bristol has now become one of the most ethnically diverse cities outside of London. Eighty-four per cent of its population is British, while 16 per cent belong to a minority ethnic group. More than ninety different languages ranging from Albanian to Vietnamese are now spoken in the city and forty-five religions are observed.

When the National Census was introduced in 1801 the total number of people living in Bristol was counted at 61,153. Ten years later it had risen to 71,483. A hundred years on, the city's population was recorded at 329,086. The 2011 census estimated the population as 428,200. An accurate figure could not be given as a number of census forms were not returned, according to officials. In the middle of 2018 Bristol's population was estimated at 463,400, with expectations that it will top the 500,000 mark in 2028 at 506,000. Another 4 million people live within an hour's drive of Bristol.

THE GREEN CITY

Bristol was named by the government in 2008 as England's first 'Cycling City'. It gave the council £11 million to encourage more cycling by creating cycle lanes on the roads and providing more training for youngsters using two wheels. The award fell in line with the council's campaign to reduce pollution by encouraging motorists to swap their cars for bicycles or public transport, or even walking to work. Six years later Bristol was chosen for the fourth stage of the Friends Life Tour of Britain. It brought to the city Sir Bradley Wiggins and 107 other top cyclists, who took to some of Bristol's steepest hills.

A major green honour came Bristol's way in 2015 when it became the first city in the United Kingdom to hold the title of European Green Capital. It was chosen from three other finalists – Brussels, Glasgow and Ljubljana, the capital of Slovenia. The award was launched in 2010 by the European Commission in recognition of the key role that local authorities play in improving and protecting the environment. Each year the award is given to a city that has a consistent record of achieving high environmental standards and is committed to further improvement. Previous winners of the title include Stockholm (2010), Hamburg (2011) and Copenhagen (2014).

Bristol has more than 450 green spaces ranging from the Clifton and Durdham Downs of more than 400 acres, to Queen Square in the centre of the city, which is just under 3 acres.

One of Bristol's key strengths in the move towards cutting pollution levels is the large number of environmental businesses now based here.

TOURISM TODAY

For many years it would have been most unusual to hear civic leaders waxing lyrical about Bristol as a major tourist centre. Indeed, when the SS *Great Britain* returned to Bristol in 1970 for restoration, one councillor publicly described it as a 'rust bucket' and others snubbed the event. Indeed, the council voted that there should not be any financial contribution towards the ship's restoration. However, five years later it agreed that the ship could remain in the docks for a peppercorn rent. The SS *Great Britain* now attracts between 150,000 and 200,000 visitors each year and plays an important role in the local tourism industry.

The tourism trade is now worth £1.4 billion to the local economy each year and supports nearly 29,000 jobs. Figures from Destination Bristol show that in 2018 there were an estimated 2.1 million staying domestic trips to Bristol, while from overseas there were 598,000 staying trips. On top of these figures there were an estimated 20.5 million day trips. To accommodate the growing number of visitors there are now forty major branded hotels, with more in the planning pipeline, in the central area of the city and on its northern fringe in South Gloucestershire. This is a huge contrast to the 1960s, when a Bristol guide book listed only ten hotels that had more than twenty rooms each.

In Bristol these days visitors are never far from a festival, whether it celebrates music, kite flying, international food, beers, cider, wine, Shakespeare or Cary Grant, the Bristol-born Hollywood star whose real name was Archie Leach. One of the biggest annual attractions is the four-day Bristol International Balloon Fiesta, first staged in 1979. The fiesta, held in the grounds of Ashton Court estate on the city's southern edge, attracts up to 150 hot air balloonists from all over the world along with 250,000 visitors. There is a riot of colour as balloons of all shapes and sizes take to the sky in the twice-daily mass ascents, weather permitting.

The annual St Paul's Carnival – a celebration of Caribbean and African culture – attracts some 40,000 visitors from all over the country to see the masquerade procession wind its way through the streets. There are also food stalls, dancing and music. St Paul's carnival was held for the first time in 1967.

The Floating Harbour has become a major recreation and tourist centre in its own right, with various events pulling in large crowds of spectators. There were thrills and spills on the water when the docks hosted international grand prix powerboat racing each year from 1971. Powerboat drivers raced around a 1¾-mile-long circuit of bends enclosed by high dock walls. Up to 250,000 spectators flocked to the city for this spectacular event. However, the curtain came down on the racing in 1991, by which time seven powerboat drivers had lost their lives.

Bristol – and possibly Britain – had seen nothing quite like the International Festival of the Sea, which was hosted in the Floating Harbour in 1996. More than 700 ships from tall ships to tiny tugs from all around the world were berthed here. For four days the city centre was full of sailors, sea salts and shanty singers. This massive sea jamboree ended with a £25,000 fireworks display and computer-controlled fountains dancing to music.

Another major event was the World Wine Fair in 1978 with twenty-nine countries taking part. It was staged in and around the docks with disused cargo sheds, specially erected pavilions and marquees along the quayside, which were used to showcase more than 1,000 different wines. A touch of Venice was brought to the harbour with a mock Rialto bridge built across St Augustine's Reach. Nearly 100,000 visitors attended the inaugural World Fine Fair over its ten-day run. It became an annual event – although not always on such a grand scale – until 1992 when it came to an end.

In the early 1970s it was unbelievable that any of these events would ever take place in Bristol for in that year an Act of Parliament was passed enabling the council to withdraw commercial shipping rights in the docks and to fill in a large section with concrete and build extensive urban roadworks instead. There was even talk of building a car park on part of the concrete-covered docks. Unsurprisingly, there was a public outcry against the scheme, which was later abandoned by the council.

SELECTED BIBLIOGRAPHY

BOOKS

Arrowsmith's Directory of Bristol, 1906.

Barnes, Max, *Bristol A–Z* (Bristol: Bristol Evening Post, 1970).

Chilcott, John, *Chilcott's Descriptive History of Bristol*, 1847 [reprinted in 2012 by General Books LLC]

Festival of Britain Souvenir Handbook, City and County of Bristol, 1951.

Green-Armytage, A.J., *Concerning Clifton* (London: J. Baker and Son, 1922).

Latimer's Annals of Bristol: Nineteenth Century, 1887.

Latimer's Annals of Bristol: Eighteenth Century, 1893.

Latimer's Annals of Bristol: Seventeenth Century, 1900.

Mathews' Bristol Directory, 1875.

Official Guide to the City of Bristol, 1924.

Ralph, Elizabeth, *Government of Bristol* (Bristol: Corporation of Bristol, 1973).

Sansom, John, *Bristol First* (Bristol: Redcliffe Press, 1997).

Sansom, John (ed.), *Children's Bristol* (Bristol: Redcliffe Press, 1966).

Sketchley's Bristol Directory 1775.

Smith, Veronica, *The Street Names of Bristol* (Bristol: Broadcast Books, 2001).

Underdown, Thomas, *Bristol Under Blitz* (Bristol: Arrowsmith, 1942).

NEWSPAPERS

Various editions of *Bristol Mirror*; *Bristol Evening Post* and its supplement the *Bristol Times* from 1932 onwards.

Western Daily Press from 1850 onwards.
Illustrated London News, December 1864.
Bristol Magpie, 1896.
Bristol Evening Post's Bristol 600 Exhibition Souvenir programme, 1973.

INDEX OF SELECTED PLACE NAMES

Also by Maurice Fells ...

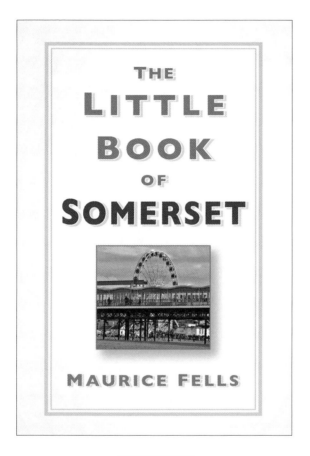

9780750987998

Also by Maurice Fells ...

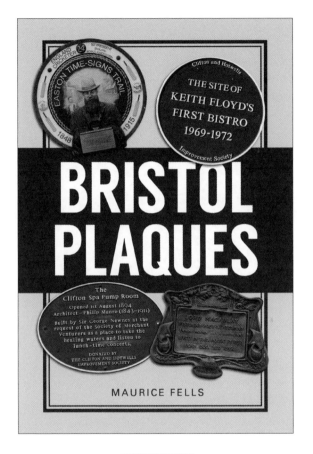

9780750965316